A reply to Doctor Wallis, his discourse concerning the Christian Sabbath by Tho. Bampfield. (1693)

Thomas Bampfield

A reply to Doctor Wallis, his discourse concerning the Christian Sabbath by Tho. Bampfield.
Defense of the Christian Sabbath.
Bampfield, Thomas, 1623?-1693.
[2], 80, [2] p.
London : Printed for Thomas Fabian ..., 1693.
Wing / B630
English
Reproduction of the original in the Cambridge University Library

Early English Books Online (EEBO) Editions

Imagine holding history in your hands.

Now you can. Digitally preserved and previously accessible only through libraries as Early English Books Online, this rare material is now available in single print editions. Thousands of books written between 1475 and 1700 and ranging from religion to astronomy, medicine to music, can be delivered to your doorstep in individual volumes of high-quality historical reproductions.

We have been compiling these historic treasures for more than 70 years. Long before such a thing as "digital" even existed, ProQuest founder Eugene Power began the noble task of preserving the British Museum's collection on microfilm. He then sought out other rare and endangered titles, providing unparalleled access to these works and collaborating with the world's top academic institutions to make them widely available for the first time. This project furthers that original vision.

These texts have now made the full journey -- from their original printing-press versions available only in rare-book rooms to online library access to new single volumes made possible by the partnership between artifact preservation and modern printing technology. A portion of the proceeds from every book sold supports the libraries and institutions that made this collection possible, and that still work to preserve these invaluable treasures passed down through time.

This is history, traveling through time since the dawn of printing to your own personal library.

Initial Proquest EEBO Print Editions collections include:

Early Literature

This comprehensive collection begins with the famous Elizabethan Era that saw such literary giants as Chaucer, Shakespeare and Marlowe, as well as the introduction of the sonnet. Traveling through Jacobean and Restoration literature, the highlight of this series is the Pollard and Redgrave 1475-1640 selection of the rarest works from the English Renaissance.

Early Documents of World History

This collection combines early English perspectives on world history with documentation of Parliament records, royal decrees and military documents that reveal the delicate balance of Church and State in early English government. For social historians, almanacs and calendars offer insight into daily life of common citizens. This exhaustively complete series presents a thorough picture of history through the English Civil War.

Historical Almanacs

Historically, almanacs served a variety of purposes from the more practical, such as planting and harvesting crops and plotting nautical routes, to predicting the future through the movements of the stars. This collection provides a wide range of consecutive years of "almanacks" and calendars that depict a vast array of everyday life as it was several hundred years ago.

Early History of Astronomy & Space

Humankind has studied the skies for centuries, seeking to find our place in the universe. Some of the most important discoveries in the field of astronomy were made in these texts recorded by ancient stargazers, but almost as impactful were the perspectives of those who considered their discoveries to be heresy. Any independent astronomer will find this an invaluable collection of titles arguing the truth of the cosmic system.

Early History of Industry & Science

Acting as a kind of historical Wall Street, this collection of industry manuals and records explores the thriving industries of construction; textile, especially wool and linen; salt; livestock; and many more.

Early English Wit, Poetry & Satire

The power of literary device was never more in its prime than during this period of history, where a wide array of political and religious satire mocked the status quo and poetry called humankind to transcend the rigors of daily life through love, God or principle. This series comments on historical patterns of the human condition that are still visible today.

Early English Drama & Theatre

This collection needs no introduction, combining the works of some of the greatest canonical writers of all time, including many plays composed for royalty such as Queen Elizabeth I and King Edward VI. In addition, this series includes history and criticism of drama, as well as examinations of technique.

Early History of Travel & Geography

Offering a fascinating view into the perception of the world during the sixteenth and seventeenth centuries, this collection includes accounts of Columbus's discovery of the Americas and encompasses most of the Age of Discovery, during which Europeans and their descendants intensively explored and mapped the world. This series is a wealth of information from some the most groundbreaking explorers.

Early Fables & Fairy Tales

This series includes many translations, some illustrated, of some of the most well-known mythologies of today, including Aesop's Fables and English fairy tales, as well as many Greek, Latin and even Oriental parables and criticism and interpretation on the subject.

Early Documents of Language & Linguistics

The evolution of English and foreign languages is documented in these original texts studying and recording early philology from the study of a variety of languages including Greek, Latin and Chinese, as well as multilingual volumes, to current slang and obscure words. Translations from Latin, Hebrew and Aramaic, grammar treatises and even dictionaries and guides to translation make this collection rich in cultures from around the world.

Early History of the Law

With extensive collections of land tenure and business law "forms" in Great Britain, this is a comprehensive resource for all kinds of early English legal precedents from feudal to constitutional law, Jewish and Jesuit law, laws about public finance to food supply and forestry, and even "immoral conditions." An abundance of law dictionaries, philosophy and history and criticism completes this series.

Early History of Kings, Queens and Royalty

This collection includes debates on the divine right of kings, royal statutes and proclamations, and political ballads and songs as related to a number of English kings and queens, with notable concentrations on foreign rulers King Louis IX and King Louis XIV of France, and King Philip II of Spain. Writings on ancient rulers and royal tradition focus on Scottish and Roman kings, Cleopatra and the Biblical kings Nebuchadnezzar and Solomon.

Early History of Love, Marriage & Sex

Human relationships intrigued and baffled thinkers and writers well before the postmodern age of psychology and self-help. Now readers can access the insights and intricacies of Anglo-Saxon interactions in sex and love, marriage and politics, and the truth that lies somewhere in between action and thought.

Early History of Medicine, Health & Disease

This series includes fascinating studies on the human brain from as early as the 16th century, as well as early studies on the physiological effects of tobacco use. Anatomy texts, medical treatises and wound treatment are also discussed, revealing the exponential development of medical theory and practice over more than two hundred years.

Early History of Logic, Science and Math

The "hard sciences" developed exponentially during the 16th and 17th centuries, both relying upon centuries of tradition and adding to the foundation of modern application, as is evidenced by this extensive collection. This is a rich collection of practical mathematics as applied to business, carpentry and geography as well as explorations of mathematical instruments and arithmetic; logic and logicians such as Aristotle and Socrates; and a number of scientific disciplines from natural history to physics.

Early History of Military, War and Weaponry

Any professional or amateur student of war will thrill at the untold riches in this collection of war theory and practice in the early Western World. The Age of Discovery and Enlightenment was also a time of great political and religious unrest, revealed in accounts of conflicts such as the Wars of the Roses.

Early History of Food

This collection combines the commercial aspects of food handling, preservation and supply to the more specific aspects of canning and preserving, meat carving, brewing beer and even candy-making with fruits and flowers, with a large resource of cookery and recipe books. Not to be forgotten is a "the great eater of Kent," a study in food habits.

Early History of Religion

From the beginning of recorded history we have looked to the heavens for inspiration and guidance. In these early religious documents, sermons, and pamphlets, we see the spiritual impact on the lives of both royalty and the commoner. We also get insights into a clergy that was growing ever more powerful as a political force. This is one of the world's largest collections of religious works of this type, revealing much about our interpretation of the modern church and spirituality.

Early Social Customs

Social customs, human interaction and leisure are the driving force of any culture. These unique and quirky works give us a glimpse of interesting aspects of day-to-day life as it existed in an earlier time. With books on games, sports, traditions, festivals, and hobbies it is one of the most fascinating collections in the series.

The BiblioLife Network

This project was made possible in part by the BiblioLife Network (BLN), a project aimed at addressing some of the huge challenges facing book preservationists around the world. The BLN includes libraries, library networks, archives, subject matter experts, online communities and library service providers. We believe every book ever published should be available as a high-quality print reproduction; printed on-demand anywhere in the world. This insures the ongoing accessibility of the content and helps generate sustainable revenue for the libraries and organizations that work to preserve these important materials.

The following book is in the "public domain" and represents an authentic reproduction of the text as printed by the original publisher. While we have attempted to accurately maintain the integrity of the original work, there are sometimes problems with the original work or the micro-film from which the books were digitized. This can result in minor errors in reproduction. Possible imperfections include missing and blurred pages, poor pictures, markings and other reproduction issues beyond our control. Because this work is culturally important, we have made it available as part of our commitment to protecting, preserving, and promoting the world's literature.

GUIDE TO FOLD-OUTS MAPS and OVERSIZED IMAGES

The book you are reading was digitized from microfilm captured over the past thirty to forty years. Years after the creation of the original microfilm, the book was converted to digital files and made available in an online database.

In an online database, page images do not need to conform to the size restrictions found in a printed book. When converting these images back into a printed bound book, the page sizes are standardized in ways that maintain the detail of the original. For large images, such as fold-out maps, the original page image is split into two or more pages

Guidelines used to determine how to split the page image follows:

- Some images are split vertically; large images require vertical and horizontal splits.
- For horizontal splits, the content is split left to right.
- For vertical splits, the content is split from top to bottom.
- For both vertical and horizontal splits, the image is processed from top left to bottom right.

ADVERTISEMENT.

There is now Printed a Book Intituled, A Treatise of the Holy Trinunity, in two Parts: The First asserteth the Deity of Jesus Christ and the Holy Spirit, in the Unity of Essence with God the Father. The Second in Defence of the former, answereth the chiefest Objections made against this Doctrine. *By I. M.*

Chap. I. The Case is briefly stated.

Chap. II. Sheweth that there is but one God, the Creator and Former of all things.

Chap. III. Asserteth a Plurality of Divine Subsistences.

Chap. IV. Of the Father.

Chap. V. Proveth the Deity of our Lord Jesus Christ. 1. By his Names. 2. That God in the Old Testament in divers Places is Christ in the New. 3. By seven particular Texts of Holy Scriptures. 4. That Christ pre-existed his Incarnation in his Divine Nature, and is no Angel incarnate, but is Coeternal with the Father. 5. His Deity is proved by his Works. And 6. By Divine Worship given to him.

Chap. VI. Proveth the Deity of the Holy Ghost. 1. That he is a Divine Person. 2. His Deity is asserted from several Texts of Scripture. 3. By his Works. 4. By Divine Worship given to him.

Chap. VII. Proveth the Unity of the Holy Trinity.

Chap. VIII. Containeth some Explications of the Holy Trinunity. 1. Of the Essential Being of God. 2. Of the Divine Persons, the Father, the Son, and the Holy Spirit. 3. Of the Distinctions of the Divine Nature and the Persons, and some Shadows by way of Comparison of the incomparable and inconceivable Being of God, and of the Union of Christ's two Natures.

PART II.

Chap. I. Answereth Objections against the Scriptural Proofs of Christ's Deity.

Chap. II. Answers to Objections drawn from several Texts of Scriptures.

Chap. III. Answers to several Arguments against the Deity of Christ.

Chap. IV. Answers to several Objections against the Scriptures, that prove the Deity of the Holy Ghost.

Chap. V. Answers to some Objections drawn from divers Scriptures to disprove the Deity of the Holy Spirit.

Chap. VI. Answers to some Scriptures from whence our Adversaries assert that the Father only is the true God. With a general Answer and Conclusion. Price bound one Shilling.

A REPLY TO Doctor Wallis, HIS DISCOURSE Concerning the Christian SABBATH.

By *THO. BAMPFIELD*.

LONDON:

Printed for *Thomas Fabian*, at the *Bible* in *Cheapside*, near *Bread-street* End, 1693.

968;01

A REPLY TO Dr. *WALLIS*'s DISCOURSE,

Concerning the

𝕮𝖍𝖗𝖎𝖘𝖙𝖎𝖆𝖓 𝕾𝖆𝖇𝖇𝖆𝖙𝖍.

SIR,

A Little after the Printing the Enquiry, Whether the Lord Jesus Christ made the World, and be *Jehovah*, and gave the Moral Law? And whether the Fourth Command be Repealed or Altered? There was Reprinted a Tract of Mr. *Chafies*, on the Fourth Command, I think, as Answer to that part of the Enquiry, which referred to the Fourth Command; and then another by one Mr. *G. T.* both which I had no sooner Examined, but another was Published by *John Wallis*, D.D.

Which Discourse of the Doctor's, as containing the strength of what is said for the First Day, I hold my self principally concerned to consider.

I find the Doctor p. 1. would not on the account of the Day, whether the Seventh or the First, give any Disturbance to the Peace or Practice of the Church where he Lives, so that a Sabbath be duly observed, tho' perhaps not upon what Day he should choose.

What

What Day he would choose, I know not, but hope it would be the Day the Lord hath Chosen and Blessed.

But the Question is not, what Day he would choose to rest upon, but what day we ought to choose, and I am willing to hope he would choose that Day, which after the best Judgment I can make upon his Book, I think, is the Seventh Day, and that he means that Day, by that, otherways Doubtful Expression.

And I think the Word is the Rule of Worship, &c. And not the Practise of the Church where we live.

Nor know I certainly what Church may be meant, for that he and I live in an Age, wherein there are variety differing a little from one another, nor am I willing to disturb the true Peace of the Churches of Christ; but if in any thing they be defective in their Judgment, or Practice, their Peace lies in their returning to their Obedience, *which is better than Sacrifice*, 1 Sam. 15. 22.

And till the Lord bring that about, I see little likelyhood the Sabbath should be duly observed, or have the full Blessing bestowed on it, which is annexed to it.

Nor do I think the true Sabbath is so hard to be found as he supposes, to whom I may say as *Moses* to the *Israelites*, Deut. 30. 11, 12, 13, 14. *This Commandment is not hid from thee, neither is it far off;* " 'Tis not beyond the Seas that we should need to go ' round the Earth to fetch it, (as the Dr. *p.* 79. pleasantly advi- ' seth) but the Word is very nigh unto thee, in thy Mouth, and ' in thine Heart, that thou mayst do it.

He says also, p. 1. *That he does not know whether* Sunday *be a first or second, a third or a seventh Day, in a continual Circulation of Weeks from the Creation, or from Christ's time*; and if so, he is at a great uncertainty, and I do not wonder if he be yet to choose his Day; which Expressions in his first Page, may give some Light to state this Question, for if he does not know from Christ's time, which Day of the Week *Sunday*, as he calls it, is, I see very little reason why he should observe it.

He adds, *And what it is impossible for him to know, he thinks will be no Crime to be ignorant of*; and if he do not know what Day of the Week *Sunday is*, and much more if it be impossible for him to know it, I see no reason at all why he should write a Book for the Observation of a Day impossible for him to know.

All

All the *Christian* and *Hebrew* Churches in the World, I think, are agreed, that *Sunday* is the first Day of the Week, which Day I presume by the rest of his Book, the Doctor observes, and if we be right in that (as I think we are) that *Sunday* is the first Day, it will be no great Task by telling seven, to resolve which is the seventh Day.

But notwithstanding the impossibility for him to know what Day of the Week *Sunday* is, he is sufficiently satisfied that we ought to keep a Sabbath, and so am I, and I think we may be sufficiently certain, which is the seventh Day in the weekly Circulation, and am willing to observe that Blessed and Sanctified Day and Time, which I think is the Lord's Day, and not changed, and so not hard to be found.

And I do not think God has left the stress of a Point, whereon his Publick Worship doth somewhat depend, upon a thing impossible for us to know; by his Word and Works, he can make this plain to all.

First, I agree with him, that the place of Worship under the Gospel, p. 2. is not so material, whether this, or that, *John* 4. 21, 23. 1 *Tim.* 2. 8. *God is a Spirit, and his true worshippers did, do, and shall worship him in spirit and in truth.* And I know no colour now for the Holiness of Places, for which yet (as the Dr. p. 3.) some are zealous.

I agree with him that *Christmas* is of Human Institution, which I think he admits by the words, *so be it*, p. 3. which I think does also lay aside all other Holy Days, which are but of Human Institution; and p. 13. about *Christmas* the Doctor says, *It is not agreed amongst Chronologies, either what Year, or what Month, much less what day of that Month our Saviour was Born*, yet (he says) *we keep* December the 25th, *in memory of his Birth, as supposing him to have been then Born*: And p. 4ʃ. he says, *No Man at this Day knows what Day it was*, and p. 13. *That we are at so great uncertainty, as we reckon the Year* 1692 *from his Circumcision to begin the first of* January, *and the same Year his Conception not till the* 25th *of* March *after*; as if his Birth and Circumcision had been a quarter of a Year before his Conception: And so the Doctor leaves those days, If I mistake not, utterly uncertain.

In p. 12. he tells us, *The Paschal Tables which should direct us what day to keep* Easter *on, do put us further out then if we had none at all.*

I agree with the Doctor, *p.* 2, & 3. that our Lord Jesus Christ according to his Divinity was God, and is so, the true God, the God that made Heaven and Earth, the God who delivered the Law at *Mount Synai*, and I think those three, *the Father, the Son, and the Holy Spirit, are on Jehovah*, Deut. 6. 4. 5. *Jehovah Ælohenu, Jehovah our Mightiest, is Jehovah Æchad, is one Jehovah, was, is, and will be one Jehovah*, (i. e.) the Lord our God, is one Lord, and Mark 12. 29, 30. *The Lord our God, is one Lord*, which are the words of Jesus.

And I agree also, that the Blessing and Sanctifying the seventh Day, Gen. 2. 3. was by *Jehovah, the Father, the Son, and the Holy Spirit*, which goes far in this Question, and I think proves the seventh Day to be the Lord's Day.

And when he has acknowledged the Father, Son, and the Holy Spirit to be three, yet but one God, the Lord *Jehovah*, &c. he adds, *p.* 3. *But he cannot agree that Christ, as God, and Man*, (in Contradistinction to the Father, and Holy Spirit) *did all those things, for he that is Christ, was not then Man.*

Which Words of the Doctor, of what he does agree, and what he cannot agree, insinuates, as if I had said, that Christ as God-Man did all those things, which the Doctor cannot agree, whereas he must needs know that is not so, for I neither say, nor ever thought (till that I read it in Mr. *G. T.* and the Doctor) that Christ was Incarnate at the making of the World, or at his giving of the Law on *Sinai*; so as the Doctor has not well surmized in this, and any Reader may see it is not so; for Christ took our Nature on him about 4000 years after the Creation: and I find not a word of any Contradistinction between the Father and the Holy Spirit, and the Son in the Enquiry, but the direct contrary, *viz.* their oneness with the Son in those Works which they both cannot but know.

And he adds, *p.* 3. what he should rather say about our Lord Jesus Christ's blessing the seventh Day, because he was not then the Lord Christ, (God and Man) *&c.* seems to make the Surmize somewhat worse, upon which he says, that I *p.* 64. la[ys] great stress) for neither I, nor any other that I know, has sa[id] or thought, that Christ, when he Blessed the seventh Day w[as] then in the Flesh, so that in this I think the Doctor blam[a]ble.

But the Doctor does acknowledge that the Son is *Jehovah*, (i. e.) that he is Lord; for which see *Enquiry, p.* 9. 10. &c. and I think he does believe that the Son of God is Jesus, that is, the Saviour, the only Saviour, and that he is Christ, that is, the anointed for that Glorious Blessed Work of Redemption, that is, the *Messiah*, he is called, as I think, often in the Old-Testament.

For the Father has chosen us in him, before the foundation of the World, in him, that is, in the Lord Jesus Christ, and our Lord Jesus Christ, as Christ, is expresly named, *Eph.* 1. 2, 3, 4.

And in *Colos.* 1. 16. speaking of Christ, *as he by whom all things were created, that are in Heaven, and that are in Earth:* v. 17. *and he is before all things,* he, that is, Christ, is expresly *Colos.* 1. 2, 3. there named the Lord Jesus Christ, and our Lord Jesus Christ, who *v.* 19. *created all things*; and Christ is named our Lord Jesus Christ in every Epistle from *Rom.* to the *Heb.* (for so far I searched a little) and that frequently, and sometime after also.

Mr. *G. T.* (whom the Doctor in this Objection seems to follow) writes of this great Mystery in two or three places under the like and greater mistakes, and so at present I leave him. But for the Doctor to impose upon his Readers herein, as he does *p.* 2, 3. seems blameable.

And why he thus begins in a Case which relates to the Deity of Christ with such Insinuations, for which he has no colour, that I know, from the Enquiry, wherein Christ's Deity and his being *Jehovah* is directly affirmed, unless it be at first to infuse some Prejudice, I am not willing to conjecture.

And as to this, if the Holy Spirit by *Paul,* names Christ the Lord Jesus Christ, and our Lord Jesus Christ, *in whom the Father hath chosen his, before the foundation of the world, by whom all things were created, and who was before all things.* I see no reason why Mr. *G. T.* and the Doctor should vary from the Apostles expressions, and divers other Scriptures. And such Artifices the Reader may discern afterward.

I agree also with the Doctor, *That God who made the world in six days, rested the seventh day,* Gen. 2. 2, 3. Exod. 20. 11. *And that he blessed the sabbath day, and hallowed* (or Sanctified) *it,* Doctor *p.* 3. *and here he does read it, not a seventh, but the seventh Day;* the same *Hebrew* word here in *Gen.* 2. 2, & 3. *Hashebigni,* which is used in *Exod.* 20. 10, 11. which some would render there a seventh; and the Reason and

Sence

sence of *Gen.* 2. 2, & 3. does require, that it be rendered as the word signifies, the Seventh Day, for no man (that I know) does imagine that the Lord, *Gen.* 2. 2, & 3. Blessed and Sanctified any other Day of the Week for Rest, but that only, on which he Rested, and that was expresly not a, but the Seventh, and no other day of the Week; and so I think, for all after Seventh days in the Circulation of after Weeks, and Christ in the time of his Incarnation kept not a Sabbath, but the Sabbath, and surely he understood his own Institution, and was not mistaken in the Day.

And the Doctor *p.* 4. says, *The Words be Blessed and Sanctified it*, may be a strong Intimation for Mankind ever after to observe the Seventh day, &c. But (he says) *is not expresly said*: And that the Seventh day Blessed and Sanctified, *Gen.* 2. 2, & 3. is not only a strong Intimation, as the Doctor, but does include the Seventh day of every Week afterward in a continual Succession, or Circulation of Days; and Weeks, I think, is proved by the Words of Blessing, and Sanctifying, or making Holy the Seventh day (which are comprehensive Words) and from *Exod.* 20. 10, 11. *as that day of every Week which Men were and are to remember to keep Holy*. And God's Sabbatizing on the Seventh day, was, as I think, that Man might keep the Sabbath day in the continual Circulation of Weeks in a Spiritual Rest.

And in this Scripture *Gen.* 2. 2. we have the Foundation for the Seventh day Sabbath, where the Words are, *And on the seventh day God had ended his work which he had made, and he rested, or sabbatized on the seventh day, from all his work which he had made*, *Heb.* 4. 4. Where it is said, he spake of the Seventh day in this wise, *and God did rest the seventh day from all his works and Elohim blessed the seventh day, and sanctified it, because that in it he had rested from all his works which God created and made*, *Gen.* 2. 3. And from God's Sabbatizing here, it is, *That the seventh day is called the sabbath*, *Exod.* 20. 9. 11. And throughout the Old and New-Testament, from the *Heb.* root *Shabath* he kept Sabbath: And the Lords Blessing the Seventh day, *Gen.* 2. 3. makes it a day of his distributing the greatest heavenly Blessings upon all that obey his Voice,

And his Sanctifying the Seventh day, shews it to be Consecrated, and so separated from all common Works, and earthly Employments, and shews it to be Dedicated and Sanctified by him,

him, to his Worship, as an Holy day, and as his day (*i. e.*) the Lords day to be used in Holy Solemn Exercises of Religion as long as the World lasts, till Believers come to that Sabbatism in Heaven, which remains for the People of God, *Heb.* 4. 4, 8, 9.

And he that doubts the Seventh day, *Gen.* 2. 2, 3. does not include every Seventh day in the continual Succession of Weeks, may see by comparing *Exod.* 20. that this Institution is not mentioned in *Exod.* 20. as then first given, but as that which God had Instituted upon his creating the World, and the keeping the weekly Sabbath, was as absolutely necessary for the Spiritual good of those Believers, and others who lived in the first Ages of the World after the Fall (and of *Adam* and *Eve* also if they had not fallen) as it is for us at this day, to Contemplate his infinite Excellencies, and mighty Works.

And *p.* 3. from *Gen.* 2. 2, 3. and *Exod.* 20. 11. he does agree, that God hath appointed (after six days of ordinary Labour) Man should observe a Seventh day of Holy rest, and this in a continual *Succession*, which I think goes far to resolve this question, not a, but the Seventh day only being first instituted, *Gen.* 2. and afterward observed as a Sabbath throughout the Scriptures.

And if he agrees (as he does *p.* 3.) that it was the Seventh day that was Blessed and Sanctified, *Gen.* 2. 3. and that this is a clear and ancient Testimony for the Holiness of time, as he doth, then, till another Sanctified Day of the Week, and another weekly time can be found which is Blessed and Sanctified by the Lord; we are (for ought I can see) to rest or keep Sabbath upon the Seventh day, as our Lord did, by whom we have no other weekly Day or Time Consecrated, or observed as Holy, but only the Seventh day, and the Doctor's opinion of the Holiness of this time has confirmed, and as I think established my Thoughts of the Holiness of the Seventh-day-Sabbath.

I agree also with him, that the Law of the Sabbath is one of the Ten Commands, *Exod.* 20. and am not only willing to think (as the Doctor) but am satisfied it was a Law before, and that not only because we find it observed *Exod.* 16. before the Law given at *Sinai*, *Exod* 20. (in which *Exod.* 16. 25, 26. the Seventh day is called a Sabbath to the Lord, (*i. e.*) the Lord's day) but especially (as the Doctor acknowledges) for that *Gen.* 2. 3.

2. 3. *God blessed the seventh day, and sanctified it*, because in it he rested from all his Work, and I do, with the Doctor, think this a clear Testimony (and as ancient as the Creation) for the Holiness of Time, (*i.e.*) as far as I can possibly discern, for the Holiness of the weekly Seventh day, for there was no other weekly Day then, or since made Holy that we can find in the Word, but the Seventh day only) and this alone will go very far to resolve and settle this question.

I agree also with the Doctor, that the Law of the Decalogue or Ten Commandments, tho' then given to *Israel*, is binding to us also, p. 3. & 4. And I think we have sufficient Evidence from the Scriptures, that the Sabbath was observed from the Creation to the Flood, tho' he thinks in the short History *Moses* gives of that time there be no mention made of such Observation from the Creation to the Flood.

For *First*, on the Seventh day God (*Heb. Elohim*) had ended his Work which he had made, and he Sabbatized on the Seventh day from all his Work which he had made, *Gen.* 2. 2.

The Example of God's keeping the first Seventh-day-Sabbath, is one undeniable Evidence of the Seventh-day-Sabbath kept after the Creation. For *Gen.* 2. 1. *The heavens, and the earth, and all the Hosts of them, were finished before the seventh day*, and so the Seventh day was kept after the Creation, and before the Flood.

A second Evidence is the same repeated, *Gen.* 2. 3. *And God blessed the seventh day, and sanctified it*, because that in it he had rested from all his Work which he had Created and Made.

Which Repetition of God's resting the Seventh day, does strongly inculcate and inforce our Duty, and certainly prove that God had rested the Seventh day after the Creation, and before the Flood.

A third Evidence from the Case of *Cain* and *Abel*, *Gen.* 4. 3. *And in process of time* Cain *brought an offering to the Lord*, and *v.* 4. Abel *also brought his offering*.

In Process of Time, *Heb. Mikketz Jammin*, at the end of Days, or at the cutting off of Days, *Enquiry* p. 23.

Which

Which end, or cutting off of days, so far as God hath revealed, seems to be the end of the Days of the Week, when the reckoning of Days was cut off, and after the Seventh day ended, they were to begin to reckon again, 1, 2, 3, 4, 5, 6, 7, and 'twas the Seventh day, the last day of the Week which before was Blessed and Sanctified, when the Creation upon the six days was finished, which Seventh day was the end of the days of the Week.

So as *Cain* (as bad as he was) and *Abel*, who obtained witness that he was righteous, *Heb.* 11. 4. both (as I think) kept the Sabbath, *Cain* outwardly, but *Abel*, no doubt, by that witness of his Righteousness, in an Holy, Spiritual, and Heavenly manner, *to whose offering the Lord had respect*, Gen. 4. 4. but to *Cain's* offering he had not respect: And if the Seventh day then ended the Week, as it now does, and if none can tell us of any other end of days at that time, I may thence infer, those offerings were at least very probably, if not certainly, upon the Seventh-day-Sabbath, and are a good Evidence for it.

And the Righteousness ascribed to *Abel*, Heb. 11. 4. surely does import his Obedience to all Gods Wills then revealed, whereof the Seventh day was eminently one, and *Abel's* sacrificing the Firstlings of his Flock was another, Gen. 4. 4.

Which Offerings were Types of Christ, and proper for the Sabbath-day, which *Abel* offered unto God by Faith, and was a more excellent Sacrifice then *Cain's*, by which *Abel* obtained witness that he was Righteous, God testifying of his Gifts, and by it, *he being dead, and yet speaketh*, Heb. 11. 4. I think he yet speaketh to us, to be Righteous as he was, and to observe the Seventh day.

And that *Abel* was a Person obedient unto God in all things, we have the Testimony of Christ, who calls him Righteous *Abel*, Matth. 23. 35.

A fourth Evidence is from Gen. 5. 22. *Enoch walked with God three hundred years.* And ver. 24. *and Enoch walked with God, and he was not, for God took him,* Enquiry, p. 23. Which *Enoch* was a Prophet, and *Jude* 14. 15. Prophesied the Lords coming to execute Judgment upon all, and to convince all that were ungodly, Greek ἀσεβεῖς all Corrupt, or all no Worshippers, thrice mentioned in the 15 ver.

C   'Tis

'Tis true, those who do not Worship God, or do not Worship him aright, are highly blameable; but the true Signification of the *Greek* word being from Alpha privative, and σέβω, to Worship: the word ασεβεῖς does tell us who they were whom *Enoch* reproved, that is, such as did not Worship God at all, or not according to his appointments, and does imply, that *Enoch* did Worship God aright, or else how could *Enoch* convince others, if himself did not keep the Blessed and Sanctified Day; and whether the word in *Jude* 14. & 15. do not imply also that the rest of the then degenerated Posterity of *Adam* whom *Enoch* reproved, did neglect the Blessed Day, seems as I conceive, very probable.

And these are Evidences for the Seventh-day-Sabbath before the Flood.

At present I pass by *Gen.* 13. 2, 3, 4, 5, 6, 9, 10. *Jashebeth*, because by the Points, it may be from the verb *Jashab*, he dwelt.

Evidences that after the Flood, the Sabbath was kept before the Law at *Sinai*.

Gen. 26. 2, 4. Enquiry p. 23. 24. the Lord appeares to *Isaac*, and promises, *that in his seed all the nations of the earth should be blessed*, ver. 5. *Because that Abraham obeyed my voice, and kept my charge, my commandments, my statutes, and my laws*. Blessing the Nations in his Seed, includes a promise of Christ upon *Abraham*'s Obedience.

How *Abraham* came to know all the Commandments, Statutes, and Laws, I know not certainly.

It may be, they being implanted in *Adam*, who was created in Gods own Image, *Gen.* 1. 26, 27. were taught down along from *Adam* in gracious Families, from Father to Son, and so to *Abraham*.

And it may be also by special Revelation; but this is certain, that *Abraham* knew these, how else could he keep or obey them; and 'tis certain he obeyed the Lords voice, and kept his Commandments, and his Laws, and one eminent Voice and Law of God was, *Gen.* 2. 2, 3. *and God blessed the seventh day, and Sanctified it*.

And *Abraham kept my Commandments*, Gen. 26. 5. and in *Exod.* 16. 27, 28. *how long refuse ye to keep my commandments*; the same *Hebrew* word with that *Gen.* 26. 5. and the Command which *Israel* brake, *Exod.* 16. 27, 28. Was that some of them,

upon

upon the Seventh-day-Sabbath went out to gather *Manna*, which they ought not to have done; and so the Command which they brake, it seems was one of those which *Abraham* kept.

And Gen. 26. 5. *Abraham kept my Laws*; and in Exod. 16. 4. The Lord to *Moses*, *I will rain bread from heaven for you, and the people shall go out and gather a certain rate every day, that I may prove them whether they will walk in my Law*, or no; and Exod. 16, 27, 28. when some brake the Sabbath, and went out to gather *Manna* on the seventh Day, the Lord says to *Moses*, *How long refuse ye to keep my laws*: it is the same Hebrew word with that Gen. 26. 5. where the Lord says, *Abraham* kept his Laws; and the Doctor does neither offer nor pretend that *Abraham* brake the Sabbath.

Now if the Law broken by the *Israelites*, Exod. 16. 4, 28. were the Seventh-day-Sabbath, as it certainly was, then 'tis very likely one of the Laws of God kept by *Abraham*, Gen. 26. 5. tho the Sabbath be not particularly there named, was the Seventh-day-Sabbath which the *Israelites* brake, Exod. 16. for we have the same Hebrew word for both, so that it does appear by Gen. 26. 5. That *Abraham obeyed the Lords voice, and kept his commandments, and his laws*; and I see no good colour to doubt it.

And he that says *Abraham* kept not the Sabbath, when God says *Abraham* kept his Commands and his Laws, may as well deny that *Abraham* kept any other of the Commands, or Laws of God; a Sixth is from Exod. 5. 5.

In Exod. 3. 18. the Lord to *Moses*, *Say to the King of Ægypt, the Lord God of the Hebrews hath met with us, and now let us go, we beseech thee, three days journey into the Wilderness, that we may sacrifice to the Lord our God;* (which they could not freely do in Ægypt) Exod. 8. 26.

Now *Horeb* (as Geographers observe) was, without hinderances, about three days Journey from *Egypt*, concerning which Mountain, God foretold *Moses*, Exod. 3. 12. *When thou hast brought forth the people out of Egypt, ye shall serve God upon this mountain.*

Upon which Mountain the Law for the Sabbath was reinforced, Exod. 20. 8.

And in Exod. 4. 21, 23. The Lord to *Moses*, *say unto Pharaoh, thus saith the Lord, Israel is my Son, and I say unto thee, let my Son go that he may serve me*:

And *Exod.* 4. 29, 30, 31. When *Aaron* had spoken to the *Israelites*, all the words which the Lord had spoken to *Moses* the people believed, and when they heard that the Lord had visited the Children of *Israel*, and that he had looked upon their Affliction, then they bowed their Heads, and worshipped; and it were not hard to say, 'tis probable that *Aarons* preaching to them all the words the Lord had spoken, and their worshipping was upon the Sabbath day, as will further appear in *Exod.* 5. 4, 5, 8, 14, 17, 19.

In *Exod.* 5. 1. *Moses* and *Aaron* went in and told *Pharaoh, Thus saith the Lord God of* Israel, *let my people go that they may hold a feast unto me in the wilderness*; and 'tis not over hard to imagine what that Feast was, which by comparing *Exod.* 14. where the Ægyptians were drowned, *Exod.* 15. 1, 22, 23. where is *Moses's* song and the murmuring at *Morah*, and *Exod.* 16. 1, 23. its likely was the Feast of the Sabbath.

Exod. 5. 2. *Pharaoh* said, *Who is the Lord that I should obey his voice, to let* Israel *go*; and ver. 3. *Moses* and *Aaron* said, *the God of the* Hebrews *hath met with us, let us go, we pray thee, and sacrifice unto the Lord our God*; and ver. 4. the King said unto them, *Wherefore do ye* Moses *and* Aaron *let the people* (or make them to cease) *from their work, get you to your burdens*; and *Exod.* 5. 5. *Pharaoh* said, *behold the people of the land now are many, and you make them rest from their burdens*.

You make them rest, *Heb. Vehishbattem*, which as I take it, is in the conjugation *Hiphil, præterit tense*, second Person, plural number, from the root *Shabath*, he kept Sabbath, and signifies, *and ye make them to keep sabbath from their burdens*, the very same root in *Gen.* 2. 2. God sabbatized, rested, or kept Sabbath on the seventh Day from all his Work which he had made, and from the same root, *Gen.* 2. 3. *and God blessed the seventh day and sanctified it: because that in it he had rested from all his work, which God created and made*. So as *Pharaoh* charges *Moses* and *Aaron* as making the *Israelites* to cease from their Work, and as making of them to keep Sabbath from their Burdens.

And when the Word of God is so plain, and full, and certain, and that by the Mouth of *Pharaoh*, an enemy that *Moses* and *Aaron* did make the *Israelites* cease from their Work, *ver.* 4. and did make them keep Sabbath, *ver.* 5. For the Doctor to say against such a plain Word (beside what was said before of *Abel, Abraham*, &c.) as he does *p.* 7. And I think sometimes afterward to

the

the like effect, that we have not the least mention of the Sabbath from *Gen.* 2. 3. 'till after *Israels* coming out of *Ægypt*, may excuse my so long insisting on these Scriptures.

So we have here in *Exod.* 5. 5. express mention of the *Israelites* ceasing from their work, and keeping the Sabbath, and the Taskmasters exacting their daily Tasks every day, *Exod.* 5. 13, 14. shews this, which are evidences for keeping the Sabbath before they came out of *Ægypt*, and *Exod.* 5. 17. *Pharaoh* upbraids them as idle, therefore ye say, let us go to do Sacrifice to the Lord.

And the Sacrifices, though they were to be offered every day, yet as a Feast-day, were offered on the Sabbath. And *Exod.* 8. 1, 8, 25, 26, 27, 28. and *Exod.* 9. 1, 13. and *Exod.* 10. 3, 7, 8, 9, 11, 22, 24, 25. are agreeable to *Exod.* 3. & 4. & 5. and *Exod.* 12. 12, 13. After the Plague upon the first Born, *Pharaoh* to *Moses* and *Aaron*, rise up, get you forth, and go and serve the Lord, as ye have said, also take your Flocks, and your Heards, as ye have said, and be gone, and bless me also. And that excellent History does shew, how the Lord delivered his people out of *Pharaoh's* hand, and all his strugling to hinder the Service of God, and to debar them of the liberty to offer Spiritual Sacrifices unto him, did all contribute to make the Deliverance more compleat, from that oppressing Bondage, sedately to serve God, and keep his Sabbaths, as in *Exod.* 16. 23. where they had a Feast of Bread from Heaven. *ver.* 4. and I think *ver.* 13. of Quails also, besides their Flocks and Heards, *Exod.* 12. 12, 13.

Another proof that *Moses* and *Aaron*, and the *Israelites* had the knowledge of the Seventh-day-Sabbath, and did observe it, and that before the Law at *Sainai*, is from *Exod.* 16.

As to the Doctor's Opinion of a new Institution of another Sabbath, *Exod.* 15. 23, 25. at *Marah*.

I answer, that upon their murmuring there because the Waters were bitter, which were there cured by a Tree which the Lord shewed *Moses*, he made a Statute and an Ordinance, and there he proved them, *ver.* 25. & 26. said, *If thou wilt diligently hearken to the voice of* Jehovah *thy God, and wilt do that which is right in his sight, and wilt give ear to his commandments, and keep all his statutes, I will put none of these diseases upon thee which I have brought upon the* Ægyptians, *for I am the Lord that healeth thee*, which seems expresly the Statute and Ordinances before mentioned,

mentioned, which Statute and Ordinance confirms the Lords Commandments, and all his Statutes, but alters none of them; so that the conceit of a new Sabbath day here instituted without any word from God, is a meer conjecture by learned Mr. *Chafie* (as afterward) and what that Statute and Ordinance was, the Doctor says, p. 4. *We cannot tell*; which I think is enough to set aside all new Epocha here. And *Exod.* 15. 27. (from *Marah*) *they came to* Elim, *where they encamped by other Waters.*

And *Exod.* 16. 1. They journyed from *Elim* to the Wilderness of Sin, and there they murmured again for want of Bread, and *Exod.* 16. 2, 3. the Lord to *Moses, I will rain bread from heaven for you, and the people shall go out, and gather a certain rate every day,* ver. 4. *And the sixth day they shall prepare that which they bring in; and it shall be twice as much as they gather daily.* ver. 5.

And at even the quails came up, ver. 13.

And every man gathered the Manna every morning, ver. 4. 21. which was every Day of the Week except the seventh Day, ver. 22.

So the Lord there reckons the days, the sixth Day and the seventh Day after the same manner as at the first, *Gen.* 1. and *Gen.* 2.

And this as it seems was not at *Elim* nor at *Marah* (but at another place and time) *viz.* in the Wilderness of Sin, which is between *Elim* and *Synai*, Exod. 16. 1. But that the Lord there altered the way of numbring the days, or instituted a new Sabbath day, no such thing is there that I can find; but reckons the sixth and seventh days (which supposes the 1, 2, 3, 4, and 5, to make up the Week) in the same manner as *Gen.* 1. and *Gen.* 2. to which seventh Day (as *Exod.* 5. 5.) the *Israelites* in *Ægypt* were no strangers.

And the Sabbath, ver. 23. is here called the Holy Sabbath, that is, the Sabbath hallowed or sanctified by the Lord, *Gen.* 2. 3. and the Sabbath is four times called the seventh Day, from ver. 26. to 30. But not a word of altering the Seventh-day-Sabbath as Mr. *Chafie* p. 31. nor any new Epocha, as the Doctor p. 10. And so the seventh Day was not forgotten, but well known to them, and yet the Doctor p. 10. tells us, *That as to the Sabbath observed from the Creation to this first raining of Manna, that there is six to one that it is not the same,* so that was uncertain also.

Nor

Nor do I see any reason why a new Epocha from *Exod.* 16. 23, 30. should be imagined, unless it be, because it is so plain a proof of the *Israelites* observing the Seventh-day-Sabbath before the Law at *Sinai*, in obedience to the Law, *Gen.* 2. 23. which answers so much of learned Mr. *Chafie*'s and of the Doctor's Books.

And if there were no new Epocha in *Exod.* 16. then it seems agreed that the seventh Day was never altered till the coming of Christ.

And the fourth Command, *Exod.* 20. 8, 11. I think puts this out of doubt.

Remember the seventh day to keep it holy, six days shalt thou labour, but the seventh day is the sabbath of the Lord thy God, ver. 9. 10. that is, the seventh Day is the Lords Day, *For in six days the Lord made heaven and earth, and rested the seventh day, and blessed the sabbath, and made it holy.*

Does any fancy that the Sabbath-day here is meant A Sabbath-day? or that the seventh-day is meant only A seventh-day, and so that another Day of the Week is intended, and will answer the letter of the fourth Command as well as the seventh-day? I answer, (beside what is said in the Enquiry) That such meaning of the fourth Command, I think is no where found in any Book before the time of Christ, nor during his Life, for such a sense would have gratified the *Jews*, to object against Christ, nor is it found whilst any of the Apostles lived; nor I think in many hundreds of years after all their deaths.

Does any doubt which is the Sabbath-day he is to remember to keep holy?

Does any doubt which is the Sabbath-day which the Lord Blessed?

Or, Does any doubt which is the Day of the Week the Lord made Holy?

The Answer is here express.

The seventh-day is the Sabbath which the Lord blessed and made holy, which we are to remember to keep holy.

Does any doubt whether the order of the Days of the Week, settled *Gen.* 1. and *Gen.* 2. was altered?

The

The answer is here plain, *For in six days the Lord made heaven and earth, and rested the seventh day*, which does refer to, and (seem to me) directly to confirm the days, and their names, of 1, 2, 3, 4, 5, 6, 7. appointed in *Gen.* 1. and *Gen.* 2. together with the time when they begin and end; and so I think we are thus far safe, that from *Gen.* 2. to *Exod.* 20. there was no new Epocha of days, nor any manner of uncertainty, which was the seventh-day; there was no intermission of the days by chance, nor the Day forgotten or neglected, as the Doctor p. 61. nor as I think any manner of doubt when the days did begin and end.

This seems to me so plain, as I had said nothing thereof, if I had not found the Doctor insist much, as if there had passed some alteration of days, and afterwards as if the Days began at Midnight, and as if I had nothing but Tradition, whereby to guess which is the seventh-day from the Creation, to *Exod.* 20. for which we have before so many highly probable, and other certain Scripture Proofs, and for which the fourth Command alone is proof enough, being declarative of what was blessed and hallowed before in *Gen.* 2. and is here in *Exod.* 20. explained and confirmed.

The Oracles of God were committed to the *Israelites*, *Rom.* 3. 2. to them was committed the keeping the Old Testament, and therein the Moral Law, and therein the fourth Command, and therein the seventh-day, and the Laws given at *Sinai*, are said to be true Laws, and good Commandments (and so they certainly were and are both true and good) and the Lord made known unto them his holy Sabbaths, *Nehe.* 9. 13, 15. and if they were made known to them, then they knew his holy Sabbaths, and if they knew them, as they did, then his Sabbaths were not altered.

And whether other Nations did measure their time by Weeks *p.* 5. See Mr. *Chafie*, chap. 13. p. 45. chap. 14. p. 49. I think expresly for it.

And to argue from *Abel*, *Enoch*, *Noah*, and *Abraham*, with such high Characters as the Lord gives them in his word, and of *Abraham* as keeping his Laws and his Commandments, are as I think strong arguments to prove the matter of fact, and sufficiently expressed that they kept the Sabbath, which is one of the Commandments, tho the Doctor *p.* 7. thinks them weak.

And

And from their Practice, and the Scriptures before cited, I think we have a certainty thereof, whereof the Doctor *p.* 8. says, *We have scarce a Conjecture, which seem hard Words against one, and yet harder against so many Scriptures.*

And tho' I am willing to thank the Doctor for what he would give me to begin the Week on *Monday, p.* 9. (that so his *Sunday* may be the Seventh-day) yet I do not think any Mans Authority so great as to alter the way of numbring the Days which God hath settled, or to controul, or alter the Day God has Blessed, and I am content with Gods Allowance and Command therein.

What is offered about the *Paschal Lamb*, and *Passover*, and *Circumcision, p.* 11. being sometimes intermitted, I think does confirm the Seventh-day, and not hurt it, for that when the *Israelites* returned to those appointments they kept them again.

And if it be true (which *p.* 13. the Doctor thinks without doubt, and certain) that we do not know which is the Seventh-day, in a continual Circulation from the Creation, then all the Doctors Arguments before and afterwards for the First day, are here as it seems without doubt, and certainly answered by himself; for if we do not know which is the Seventh day, we cannot know which is the First day, and so cannot possibly keep a Day which we know not; and somewhat like this he offers *p.* 1. Nor do I see how the Doctor or any other Person can be long held to think as they seem to do.

And *p.* 1. He thinks it impossible for him to know the First day, and *p.* 14. Impossible for any Man to know the Seventh day, which are also directly against him.

And *p.* 16. he says, *We have no particular Command in another Case*, which I think we have, and not only a practice, most likely to be Gods Will, *p.* 17. But that not being now in question, I pass it by.

And as to what he there says for the change of the Seventh to the First day, that I would think so also if I were not otherwise prepossed with Prejudice, and with a great fondness to find out somewhat wherewith to find fault.

I Reply, that I doubt we have many great Faults not hard to be found, and I commend to the Doctor *Rev.* 3. 17. But I know nothing of Prejudice or Fondness, corrupt Nature and human Frailties, by Grace disallowed in this, and all Cases excepted, as he surmises; but whensoever I find in the Scriptures

D any

any Truth which would correct my Conversation, and make it agreeable to Gods Will, after due search and consideration honestly and conscientiously to comply with it, as other Christians do or ought; and this question has been considered by me now near twenty six Years.

And if such Truth, according to the best of that Knowledge God hath graciously given concern others also, then to communicate it, and if it be a Truth, which can be by me no other way opened to them, then to do it in this sort, as I weakly can, and I shall be heartily glad the Doctor or any other would do it much better, as he is very well able.

And if we are not to hide our selves from our Brother's Ox, or his Sheep when we see them go astray, *Deut.* 22. 1, 2, 3, 4.

And if we are obliged when others, especially our Brethren, err in Judgment or Practice to reprove them, How much more are we bound when we see many erring in a moral Duty, to endeavour to set them right?

And to surmise upon him that he writes those Reflections, and many others, to prepossess and prejudice Readers I am loath to do.

Nor had I made this Vindication if I had not been compelled by the Doctor's Charge.

And as to the *Israelites* keeping the true Seventh-day-Sabbath commanded *Exod.* 20. from thence to the Incarnation of our Lord, I do not remember the Doctor to deny it; for which I think there is enough said in the *Enquiry*, *p.* 26. 27, 28. and much more might be added if need were; and I am unwilling to write again the same things, altho' by repeating the same Objections, and reinforcing the old with new Words; I am sometime constrained so to do.

And in general I say, that as far as I can judge, there is enough said in the Enquiry to prove that (not A, but) The Sabbath Instituted *Gen.* 2. and Repeated *Exod.* 20. and observed from thence to Christs coming, and (with every tittle of the rest of the Moral Law) confirmed, and made perpetual by Christ in *Matth.* 5. 17, 18, 19. and *Luke* 16. 14, 17. who certainly knew the true Sabbath day, binds all men, till the Heaven and Earth pass away, which is not yet.

And

And (not A Seventh day, but) The Seventh day there established, and made perpetual, was observed by Christ, during his Life, for so was his custom, *Luke* 4. 16, to 21. *Enquiry*, p. 38. 39, 41, 42, 43, 45. and was observed by Believers after his Death, Resurrection, and Ascension; so was *Paul's* custom, *Acts* 17. 2. which was never altered by the Word that I know.

Which confirming and making the Law perpetual, and every Jot and Tittle of it by Christ, who was and is Jehovah, does also fully prove (as I think) that (not A, but) the Seventh-day-Sabbath was neither altered, nor changed, nor forgotten, nor any way uncertain to Christs time, neither as to the day, nor as to the beginning or ending of it, and that the Seventh day is the Lords Day.

This being premised, let us consider what the Doctor further offers for the First, or against the Seventh day; *p*. 17. 18. he tells us, *That Christ on the day of his resurrection, did not only appear to the good Women at the Sepulchre, and declare to them the Resurrection, but also the same day himself declares it to two of them going to* Emmaus, *Luke* 24. 27, 32. *and did expound to them in all the Scriptures, the things concerning himself, and did open to them the the Scriptures, and did* (as he takes it) *celebrate the Lords Supper,* implyed in the words, *he took bread, and blessed it, and brake, and gave to them,* ver. 30, &c.

'Tis true, Christ after the Resurrection, appeared to *Mary Magdalen*, and to the other *Mary*, *Matth.* 28. 1. 9.

And the Angel said to them, *v.* 5. and *Mark* 16. 5, 6. *He is not here but is risen, go tell his disciples that he is risen from the dead, which they did, but the Disciples believed them not*.

Now 'tis certain, as 'tis agreed, that Christ rose the Third day, which Third day was the First day of the Week; and that the Angel *Matth.* 28. 5. (and two Angels *Luke* 24. 4. and *John* 20. & 12.) said to the Women, *that Christ was risen, and the women told it to the Disciples, yet the Disciples would not believe them;* and we have Christ appearing to two Disciples as they travelled into the Country, *Mark*. 16. 12. *And they went and told it to the rest of the Disciples, but they believed not them,* Verse the 13.

And Christ's appearing to the Women, was a practical proving of the Resurrection.

Some think the two Disciples, *Mark* 16. 12. to be the two Disciples traveling to *Emmaus*, *Luke* 24. 13. which is very likely, and that *Peter* from *Luke* 24. 34. and 1 *Cor*. 15. 5. was one of them. But 'tis certain they were two Disciples, and yet the rest would not believe them, *Mark* 16. 13.

And their Discourse upon the way as they travelled together, *Luke* 24. 13. was such as the Doctor mentions, and Christ there reproved them for not believing what the Prophets had spoken, *v.* 25. That Christ ought to suffer, but did not reprove them that we read, for travelling on that day.

And 'tis likely the Breaking and Blessing of Bread, *ver.* 30. might be (for ought I know) the Sacrament of the Supper, and implied.

But still the Journey from *Jerusalem* to *Emmaus*, and back again was a travelling Journey, being near fifteen Miles, and more then a Sabbath days Journey, as the Doctor agrees; and I do not see how he can make that Journey consist with the keeping that First day as a Sabbath, whereof there is there, or before no Institution, nor any Mention, but rather the direct contrary; their travelling upon that First day of the Week (without any reproof from Christ) as upon any other of the Six days, seems directly against the Doctor.

And whether our Lord did then travel without pain (as the Dr.) is not written; he had then the Wounds in his Body, and at his appearing afterward to the Disciples, and *Thomas*, *John* 20. 25, 27. *Luke* 24. 29. and yet might be without pain, for ought I know, but surely the two Disciples travelled as others do.

And although the Disciples were eminently Holy, yet because not written, I do not know what they were then imployed about at *Jerusalem*, (unless it were mourning and weeping, *Mark* 16. 10.) (where they were assembled for fear of the Jews, *John* 20. 19.) before or after the report of the Women, whom they did not credit.

And *p*. 19. I think the Doctor agrees the meeting of the Disciples there providential, and not upon a Sabbath account, for 'twas for fear of the Jews.

And Christs appearing to the Eleven as they sat at Meat, *Mark* 16. 14. agrees therewith, it was as they sat at Meat.

And

And to what he offers p. 19. from *Luke* 24. 36. & 42. and *John* 20. 19. our Lords appearing to the Disciples at *Jerusalem*, and saying, *peace be unto you*. So *Mark* 16. 14, 15, 16. I answer, this Salutation of Peace be unto you, or such like, is frequent in the Scriptures, and must be strangely and strongly forced to speak any thing of instituting the First day.

The Resurrection was and is a great Truth, and necessary to be known and assured, and yet the Disciples were unbelieving of it, notwithstanding all that Christ told them before his Death, *Mark* 9. 31. *That he should be delivered into the hands of Men, and be killed, and after that rise the third day*, as *Mark* 10. 33, 34. *Luke* 24. 7, &c.

And his Resurrection was proved to them by several Witnesses, *Luke* 24. 10. whose words seemed to them as Idle tales, v. 11. and the Lord himself upbraides them for their hardness of heart, because they believed not them who had seen him after he was risen, *Mark* 16. 14. So it became necessary (if I may so say) for the Lord to give full and undeniable Evidence of the Truth of his Resurrection, by his Personal appearing to the Eleven upon the very day thereof, as he did, as they sat at Meat, *Mark* 16. 14. that there might be no room left for any doubt of his being actually risen from the Dead. A Truth upon which the whole Doctrine of the Gospel did, and does eminently depend; and this I think is a fair account of our Lords appearing to the Disciples at *Jerusalem*.

But that this did alter the Seventh, or appoint the First day for a Sabbath, I find not, but seems all dark Conjecture, without any warrant from the Scriptures.

And yet the Doctor p. 20. says, *all which being put together, seems to him very like the Celebration (if not the Consecration) of a Christian Sabbath, or day of Holy Rest, and Religious Service*.

I fully acknowledge, that all that was spoken by our Lord, as well before as after his Resurrection, was Spiritual and Heavenly, upon all the Sabbaths he kept as his Custom was, and at all other times before and after his Resurrection, but yet, that that which the Doctor allows, as it seems to me, as providential, and not upon a Sabbatical account should alter the Seventh day, or institute the First, I see not.

And we do not read the Lord blaming his Disciples for resting upon the Sabbath day, or for travelling upon the First, but for their not believing his Resurrection.

So

So as the Seventh-day-Sabbath (by all the Doctor has yet offered) seems not hurt.

From *John* 20. 26. *After eight days Christ appeared to the Disciples, and* Thomas *with them.*

Christ had appeared to the Eleven Disciples at Evening upon the day of his Resurrection, as they sat at Meat, *Mark* 16. 14. which was the First day of the Week, *John* 20. 19. when they were assembled for fear of the Jews, but *Thomas* not being there *John* 20. 24. *would not believe, unless he should thrust his hand into his side,* ver. 25.

And after eight days, Christ appeared to the disciples, and Thomas *with them*, John 20. 26. and saith to *Thomas, reach hither thy hand, and thrust it into my side, and be not faithless, but believing,* ver. 27. which was an admirable Condescension of our Lord to cure his, and all others unbelief.

Those Words after eight Days, the Doctor thinks was that day seven-night, &c. *The Cavil,* for so the Doctor calls it, he says, *is so weak, that he is sorry to see it,* p. 20. And then takes great pains to prove, *That after eight days* (as we commonly speak in *English,* on that day seven-night) *is the next First day after the Resurrection.*

I have perused the *Enquiry,* p. 50. 51. that after eight days is not that day seven-night. and I neither discern it to be a Cavil, nor so weak as the Doctor represents it; but that after eight days may be, as it seems to me, the second or third day seven-night after the Resurrection.

In *Matth.* 26. 2, 6, 14, 16, 17. *after two days was the passover,* seems to be meant, *after two days exclusively,* (i. e.) *excluding the day on which that was said.*

Rev. 11. 11. *After three days and an half,* about the two witnesses, *the spirit of life from God entred into them, and they stood upon their feet,* is understood as I think, with Reason, after not two, but three Days, or Years, and an half expired, God will revive them, and restore them to his Service, and 'tis the same Greek word for, after, here, as *John* 20. 26. So after eight days, may not include the day wherein 'twas spoken, and so may be the second or third day seven-night after.

And I do not know that ever I heard, much less do we commonly so speak, that after eight days is that day seven-night after, or that after eight days, does include the day wherein it is so said for one of the eighth days, and if it did include it yet after eighth seems to be the ninth, and that in *John* 20. 26. was also spoken in the Evening, (*i. e.*) near the end of that day.

As for what the Doctor offers, that after eight days must be that day seven night, because Christs rising the third day, is said in *Mark* 8. 31. to be after three days.

I say the Crucifixion was upon the sixth day, the Resurrection upon the first Day of the next Week, which does explain what is meant by after three days, *Mark* 8. 31. that is, after part of the Sixth day, the whole seventh Day, and part of the First day.

Now, when after three days, is so explained in divers Scriptures to be the third day, it may not follow, that after eight Days, which is no where that I know, so explained, must include the Day spoken in, and exclude the day after the Eighth.

And that the Resurrection was upon the third day, I think there is enough offered in the *Enquiry*, see *Matth.* 6. 21, & 17. 23, & 20. 19, & 27. 64. *Mark* 9. 31. & 10. 34. *The words of our Lord, The Son of Man shall rise again the third day, Luke* 9. 22, & 13. 32, & 18. 33, & 24. 7, & 21. 46. 1 *Cor.* 15. 4. *He rose again the third day,* so as the Resurrection was on the third Day, and the words, after three Days, are fully explained to be the third Day, or in, on, or upon the third Day, and the first of these three Days is expresly included.

And μετὰ, after, sometimes signifies, in, and *Mark* 8. 31. rendred in three Days, answers that Objection, and the Enemies *Matth.* 27. 64. desired *Pilate* that the Sepulchre might be secured untill the third Day, that is, till the third Day is come, not till after the third Day is past, and so the Enemies understood the Resurrection would be in or on the third Day, and all Scholars know that.

Greek Prepositions and Particles, are often variously rendered, as the reason of the place where they are used does require.

And if this place in *Mark* 8. 31. be so rendered in three Days, (*i. e.*) after the third Day is come, that agrees with all the above cited Scriptures, for his rising the third Day; and so *Grotius* and *Beza*, and other Annotators on *Mark* 8. 31.

And

And there is this difference as before, that *after eight days* is no where explained to be the eighth day, including the first of the eight, or excluding the day after the eighth, nor explained by, *in eight days*, as *after three days*, in *Mark* 8. 31. is expresly explained by many Scriptures to be the third day, (and as above in three days (*i. e.*) till the third day).

What is offered *p.* 22. from *Luke* 1. 59. on the eighth day they came to Circumcise *John*, was according to the Institution, *Gen.* 17. 12. *He that is eight days old shall be circumcised*, which Institution does actually include the day of Birth, for that the day of Birth is one day, and seven days more do accomplish eight days, *Luke* 2. 21. but 'tis no where said of that (that I know) that 'twas after eight days that they were to be Circumcised.

But if *after eight days* did include the first of the eight days, and did exclude the day after the eighth day, yet here is no abrogating the Seventh-day-Sabbath, nor any instituting the first day, not any word to any such purpose; but this seems an occasion taken by our Lord (after eight days after his Resurrection) when *Thomas* was with the rest of the Disciples who was not present at Christs first appearing to them, to cure his unbelief, and to confirm the Faith of the rest of the Disciples, and of all others, in these two great Doctrines, one of the Deity of Christ, whom *Thomas* there openly and expresly owns to be the Lord his God, *My Lord, and my God*, John 20. 28, 29.

The other of the Resurrection of Christ, which till then *Thomas* said, *he would not believe*, John 20. 24, 25. In which two great Doctrines the rest of the Disciples were before confirmed, as in the *Enquiry*.

From *p.* 23. to *p.* 28. the Doctor would make the day begin at mid-night, and to end at mid-night, according to the Roman account, and that to be the Evening and the Morning, *Gen.* 1ƒ. and from mid-night to mid-night to be the day.

And though I am not willing to contend about terms, what is the Natural, and what the Artificial day, yet I may not admit the Days of the Week to be any other than what God first fixed in the Scriptures, that is the Evening, and the Morning. 'Tis true, the Day as distinguished from the Night begins in the Morning, and ends in the Evening; and the Night, or Darkness, as distinguished from Day, begins in the Evening, and ends

in

in the Morning, but the whole day confifted of Evening and Morning, that is, of Night and Day; and we find *Gen.* 1. 3. that when Light was Created, *Let there be light.* Ver. 4. *God divided the light from the darkneſs.* Ver. 5. *And God called the light Day, and the darkneſs he called Night: and the evening and the morning were the firſt day:* And ſo the Light was the Day, and Darkneſs the Night, as diſtinguiſhed from one another; but one Day, or the Firſt Day of the Week, confifted of Evening and Morning, that is, of Darkneſs and Light, which was the Firſt day. And ſo *Ver.* 8. *the evening and the morning were the ſecond day*; and *ver.* 13. *the evening and the morning were the third Day*; and *ver.* 19. *the evening and the morning were the fourth Day*; and *ver.* 23. *the evening and the morning were the fifth Day;* and *ver.* 31. *the evening and the morning were the ſixth Day*; and the ſeventh day God reſted, or Sabbatized, *Gen.* 2. 2, 3. where Seventh day is thrice mentioned, *And God bleſſed the ſeventh day, and ſanctified it,* or made it Holy: which making it Holy, I think, refolves the main Queſtion, which Days of the Week, confifting of Evening and Morning, that is, of Darkneſs and Light, and ſo beginning in the Evening, and ending the Evening after, is there appointed and fixed, and material and plain, and may not be altered. And our manner of reckoning of days here, I think is not in queſtion now between us.

P. 22. He takes notice about what time, *Mary Magdalen* came to the *Sepulchre,* on the day of Chriſts Refurrection.

And upon *Luke* 23. 55, 56. When they beheld the *Sepulchre,* and how the Body was laid, the Doctor ſays, that was on the ſixth day at night, (which (night) I cannot find in the word that it was at Night) and they returned, and prepared Spices and Ointments, and reſted the Sabbath day according to the Commandment; which is true, that they returned, prepared Spices, reſted, and kept the Sabbath, which was not A, but the Seventh-day-Sabbath after the Death of Chriſt; whilſt his Body was in the Grave, and he in Paradice (*i. e.*) in Heaven. But I know no word for that, that Chriſt was buried in the Night, but towards the end of the ſixth Day, and if it were not at Night, the Doctor ought not ſo to write.

And from *Luke* 24. 1. *Matth.* 28. 1. *Mark* 16. 1. *John* 20. 1. The Doctor would observe, *p.* 23. that the Sabbath according to their Account, did not end till towards the Morning of the next day, but it being not said in either of those places or elsewhere, that I find in the word, that the Sabbath did not end till towards the Morning, but that Christ was risen when the Sabbath was past, *Mark* 16. 1. *Early in the morning of the first day*, ver. 2. This proves against him, as I think, that the Sabbath was ended before, *viz.* the Evening before.

And yet the Doctor says it is manifest, that at this time, as well the Sabbath as other days, were by them reckoned not from Evening to Evening, but rather according to the Roman account, from mid-night to mid-night.

And to prove it, says, *it was sometime after the ninth hour* ((i. e.) our three a Clock in the Afternoon) that Christ gave up the Spirit, *Mark* 15. 34, 37. and later, when they brake the Thieves Legs; and later, when *Joseph* begged his Body, took it and buried it, by which he would prolong the time to run it up into the Night, for which Night we find no Word, and for which I see no Reason, nor know any other to whom his sence of this prolonged time is manifest, the general sence of Learned Cristians being as I think against him. All those things being well consistent before the Sabbath drew on, and our Lords giving up the Spirit, the begging of his Body, taking it and burying it, in a Tomb prepared, might all be in a very little time, for *John* 19. 42. *The sepulchre was nigh at hand*, which surely was so little time as to be all finished upon the Sixth day, before the Sabbath drew on, *Luke* 23. 54, 55, 56. And for the Women to prepare Spices and Ointments the same Sixth day, and all before the Sun set.

And this way of the Doctor's reasoning, if it would hold, which I think it will not, would break in upon the Sabbath, upon which the Women rested according to the Commandment, *Luke* 23. 56, &c. and would leave a doubt, whether the Sixth day were one of the Three days, unless men believe as the Doctor, that the days begin at mid-night; see Mr. *Shepherd's* Tract on this Subject.

The general opinion I think is right in this, that the reckoning of days in the time of the Old Testament was from Evening to Evening, which reckoning I find not yet altered in the Word;

Word; but the *Romans*, who were then Heathens, did reckon days from mid-night to mid-night.

And *p.* 24. how long the First day lasted is built on a Foundation, as if the day began at mid-night.

And *p.* 25. he says, *We reasonably suppose from* Luke 24. 29, 30, 35. *that the two Disciples from* Emmaus *came pretty late at night to* Jerusalem.

Which is but supposed, not in the Word, which Word is the Wisdom of God, and the highest Reason.

Ver. 29. They said to Christ, *abide with us, for it is towards evening, and the day is far spent,* which might, and surely did leave time enough for them to return to *Jerusalem* that day; for *Luke* 24. 33. *They rose up the same hour, and returned to* Jerusalem, which intimates their haste in returning to *Jerusalem*.

And 'twas the same Day of the Resurrection, that is, the First Day of the Week, at Evening, that our Lord appeared to the Disciples at *Jerusalem*, *John* 20. 19. as they sat at Meat, when the Doors were shut where the Disciples were assembled for fear of the Jews, upon the First day at Evening, and *John* 19. 40, 41, 42. The Body of Jesus was laid in a Garden, because of the Jews Preparation day, for the Sepulchre was nigh at hand, and so no need of much time to bury him, all was easie to be finished before the Sabbath began, to which the Sixth day was a Preparation day, which proves it to be the day before the Sabbath; yet the Doctor thinks it was about mid-night, and then infers as manifest, that the Jews and four Evangelists did reckon their days from mid-night to mid-night, and there adds, if they did not so reckon, Christ could not be sa'd, *Matth.* 12. 40. to be three Days and three Nights in the heart of the Earth, which I take it, is not well said, for to make a doubt of the three Days in the Grave, unless we believe it manifest, that the Jews and four Evangelists did reckon their days from mid-night to mid-night, seems very blamable.

The Doctor thinks *p.* 26. the days in the time of the Old Testament, reckoned from mid-night to mid-night; and from *Exod.* 12. 6, 14, 15, 16. about the Passover that Evening *v.* 6. (or as in the Margent, between the two Evenings) is at mid-night, and that assoon as mid-night is past, Morning began, and says the account thereof, is so fair, as we need not scruple to embrace it.

And

(28)

And he thinks from the first born of *Egypt* being slain at midnight, that, the midnight began the next day after the Passover, then which he thinks nothing can be more clear, and p. 28. takes it to be very plain from what he has said, *That at the time of Christs Death and Resurrection, the days were counted from midnight to mid-night,* which matters which he thinks plain, clear, and manifest, I think are mistaken by him.

What was offered from *Gen.* 1. 5. the Evening and the Morning were the First day, the Doctor thinks is easily answered, and renders it as in the *Hebrew,* and the Evening was, and the Morning was, one day (*i. e.*) says he, *there was in the First day, and so in the rest, Evening and Morning, or Darkness and Light,* which is so far true; and says, *Darkness is put first, because* (beginning the Day from mid-night) *the Dark is before the Light;* but if it were so, which I think is not, then the Darkness would be after the Light, *viz.* till mid-night after, and would put Night and Day in Confusion.

To which I further say, as he, by day one, or one day, *Gen.* 1. 5. is there meant the First day; and so I think in the New-Testament, by μία, one day is generally meant the first day, and the first day is certainly meant, as to the day of Christs resurrection.

But that the Evening in *Gen.* 1. 5. began at midnight, is contrary to the current of learned men (Doctor *p.* 26.) and contrary to Mr. *Chasie,* and contrary to the *Hebrews,* who best knew the meaning of the Books of *Moses,* and I think contrary to the Scriptures throughout, which begin the Evening when the Sun does set, *Mark* 1. 32. whereof more by and by.

And as to the Evenings, *Exod.* 12. 6. it seems to me, that one, or the First Evening, was the Evening, which (after the Sun created) began the days (*i. e.*) when the Sun did set, and the other Evening was about the time of the daily and weekly Sacrifices, which ordinarily, I think, was about their ninth Hour, (*i. e.*) our three a Clock in the Afternoon, which *Acts* 3. 1. is called the ninth Hour, the Hour of Prayer, when *Peter* and *John* went to the Temple.

So *Cornelius* in a Vision, saw an Angel about the ninth Hour, *Acts* 10, 3. And the ninth Hour, that is, our three a Clock in the Afternoon, was about the Hour of our Saviours being made a Sacrifice for his People, *Matth.* 27. 46. *Mark* 15. 34.

Or that other Evening might be, *1 Kings* 18. 29, 36. when Mid-day was past.

And (betwixt the two Evenings, *Exod.* 12. 6.) is understood by many, to be betwixt the declining of the Sun after Noon, and the setting of the Sun, which may well be; but the first Evening began at Sun set, and belonged to the Day of the Week, which Days of the Week consisted of Evening and Morning, as before.

Their Morning-Worship seems to have been about our nine a Clock in the Morning, which I think was their third Hour, *Acts* 2. 4, 15. at which Hour the Holy Spirit was poured out.

But the Evening of the Days of the Week after the Sun created, I think began at, or about Sun set, and comprehended from Sun setting to Sun rising, and the Morning, from Sun rising to Sun set, which Evening and Morning made up every day of the Week then, and ever since as before.

And yet the Doctor *p.* 25. thinks, that both the Jews and four Evangelists did reckon their days from mid-night to mid-night.

And the *Paschal Lamb, Exod.* 12. 3, 6. which was to be killed the Fourteenth day of the first Month, between the two Evenings, *Exod.* 12. 2, 6. (whether the Evening wherein they were to kill it began at our three a clock in the Afternoon, or presently after Noon) gave them time enough to kill it and dress it, without running up the time to mid-night.

'Tis true, *The Lord smote the first-born of* Ægypt *at mid-night*, ver. 29. and why it was at mid-night I know not, but (if we may so humbly say) it might be (*inter alia*) for greater terror to Ægypt.

Which mid-night there, did not that we find, alter the institution of the Passover, much less did that smiting the *Ægyptians* alter the Days of the Week; and so our Lord observed the Passover before his Passion with his Disciples the Fourteenth Day of the first Month at Even, *Matth.* 26. 20. *Mark.* 14. 17. *Luke* 22. 7, 14.

And we read, at Even there was upon the Tabernacle, as it were, the appearance of Fire, untill the Morning, and so it was alway, and so the Evening did not here begin at mid-night, but as it began to be dark, *Numb.* 6. 9, 15, 16, 21. that is, when the Sun did set.

Which

Which Fire gave Light when it was Dark, that is, from the Evening till the Morning.

And that the Evening does begin, not at mid-night, but at Sun set, we have many places in the Old and New-Testament, *Deut.* 23. 11. When the Evening cometh on, is, when the Sun is down; they are the words of *Moses*, who wrote *Genesis* and *Deuteronomy*.

And *Josh.* 10. 26, 27. *The five Kings were hanged on five trees until the evening, and at the time of the going down of the sun, they took them down by* Joshua's *command*; so as the Evening was the time of the Suns going down in *Moses* and *Joshua*'s time.

In *Prov.* 7. 9. the Evening is called the Twilight, in the Twilight in the Evening of the Day, and the Twilight begins when the Sun sets.

Jer. 6. 4. *The day goeth away, for the shadows of the evening are stretched out*; now when the Sun sets the Earth begins to be shadowed, and then the former day goeth away.

Mark 1. 32. *And at even when the sun did set, they brought to him all that were diseased,* or the Evening being come when the Sun had set, which makes it as plain as words can well express it, that the Evening began not at mid-night, but when the Sun did set, and that when *Mark* wrote his Gospel.

So *Mark* 13. 35. The Words of Christ, *Watch, for ye know not when the master cometh, at even, or at mid-night, (or at cock-crowing, or in the morning)* so the Even was one time, and midnight another, so the Evening did not begin at mid-night, and yet the Doctor thinks it manifest, and that we need not scruple to embrace it, then which he thinks nothing can be more clear, whereas it seems very plain by the Scriptures, that every day begins in the Evening, that is, when the Sun sets.

And if it be so as above, then all which the Doctor says for mid-night-day, and all he builds thereon fails, which may confirm us that the Crucifying of Christ was on the Sixth day of the Week, about our three a Clock in the Afternoon, and that the Resurrection was upon the First day of the Week in the Morning; and yet the Doctor *p.* 28. thinks it to be very plain, that at the time of Christs Death and Resurrection, the Day began at mid-night, and did continue till mid-night.

And in p. 28. says, *We have now found our Saviours Example as to the two first Sundays from his Resurrection*; if at least their First day of the Week be our Sunday, for the uncertainty of the days, which is the First, and which is the Seventh day he still holds, as before, as I think, against himself, for if our Sunday be not the First day, why does he plead for it?

By which, frequent reserve of the uncertainty which is the First day of the Week, if the Doctor does mean to rebuild the First day (as the Romanists, and some few others) upon the authority of the Church, or of the Civil Magistrate, it seems fair to tell us so, for if it be uncertain what day of the Week the First day is, I cannot see any Foundation in the Word, or common Reason for observing an uncertain weekly Day, and if it be uncertain, then it is certainly gone.

As to our Saviours Example which the Doctor has found, as to one of those two First Sundays, it is an Example of our Saviours, and two of his Disciples travelling on Sunday, which Example I may allow him, without any hurt or danger to the main question.

And his other Example, about, after Eight days, which he has found, has been answered, as I think before.

And these two Sundays, are all that the Doctor finds as Examples by Christ, for altering the Sabbath from the Seventh to the First day, of which altering we find not one word in either.

He says nothing of any Word or Example of Christ before his Death, for such alteration, for he knows our Saviours manner was to keep the Sabbath during his Life.

Nor says he, that I remember, any thing of the Thief, his being with Christ in Paradice the same day of his Crucifixion, *Luke* 23. 42, 43.

Then *p.* 29. he says, *We have clear Evidence of a like Practice*, *Acts* 20. 7. And so leaps over all about *Paul*, and others keeping the Sabbath, that is in the former Chapters of the *Acts* of the *Apostles*, which I shall have occasion to remember him of.

From which *Acts* 20. 7. he renders *dielegeto*, holding forth, and this rendring holding forth, the Doctor does twice, *page* 29.

In the *Enquiry*, p. 55. in anſwer to the Objection from *Acts* 20. 7. where *Paul* Preached to the Diſciples, I take notice, that the Greek Word there rendred Preached, is in *Acts* 17. 2. rendred Reaſoned, where *Paul*, as his manner was, Preached to them three Sabbath-days; and ſo the ſame Greek word with that in *Acts* 20.7. is rendred Reaſoned in *Acts* 18.4. where *Paul* Preached in the Synagogue every Sabbath, to Jews and Gentiles, this little notice I take of the ſame Greek word in theſe three places of *Acts* 20. 7. *Acts* 18. 4. and *Acts* 17. 2. rendred Preached, *Acts* 20. 7. but rendred Reaſoned, *Acts* 18. 4. and *Acts* 17. 2. Though it be the ſame Greek word which I think of ſome uſe to ſhew that *Paul* preached Chriſt every Sabbath, the Doctor ſeems to take offence at, and gives leave to render it, *Paul did bold forth*, and inſtead of, *he continued his Speech, that he held on his bolding forth*, till mid-night, which Expreſſion of holding forth has been much abuſed in this Age by ſome Men, againſt eminently Holy and Learned Non-conforming Miniſters, when they have been accuſed as Malefactors for Preaching the Goſpel, to ſcorn, reproach, and deſpiſe them as holders forth, &c. And the Expreſſion of Holding forth being taken in an ill and deſpightful ſence by ſome, who ſo uſe it.

I think the Doctor might have ſpared to put it upon *Paul*, who in his Preaching Chriſt, was then a Non-conformiſt Miniſter, and Preacher.

And it ſeems, if it were not written incauteloufly to be highly blamable.

In which Expreſſions of Holding forth, with others afterward, which refer to Spiritual Praying and Praiſing, as this does to Preaching the Goſpel. The Doctor goes in bad company, and I doubt, highly gratifies them, whilſt he writes ſo agreeably to their Language.

Which words of the Doctor, however written with ſome ſeeming ſoftneſs, are a very ill Bleat if they were meant, which I hope they were not, as they are commonly underſtood by all good and bad Men that I know.

And in further Reply to the Doctor's from *Acts* 20. 7. I refer to what is in the *Enquiry*, p. 55. 56, 57, 58.

And admitting that (one) there is one day, and that one day the Firſt day of the Week, and that the Diſciples there came together to break Bread, and admitting that breaking of Bread was the Lords Supper, and the Aſſembly there to be a Chriſtian Aſſembly,

Assembly as it was, yet supposing the day as before, does not begin at mid-night, but in the Evening, as I think it certainly doth; and supposing *Paul* as his manner was *Acts* 17. 2. (as before) preached on the Sabbath, every Sabbath, *Acts* 18. 4. *Acts* 16. 30. and that to Jews and Gentiles, *Acts* 13. 14, 42, &c. which cannot be denied; and supposing that what we have in the Prophets reproving *Israel* for prophaning, or polluting (as *Esai.* 56. 2, 4, 6. *Esai.* 58. 13, &c.) the Sabbath, or any part thereof, to be generally expressed by their refusing to keep the Sabbath, and supposing what we have in the New-Testament about our Lords custom of keeping the Sabbath to be briefly expressed, (by his going into the Synagogue on the Sabbath, and as preaching) does comprehend, and include all the rest that was requisite to the perfect keeping the Sabbath, as it certainly did, or else we should have read it there objected against him, which we do not find; and supposing the like of the Apostles in their measure in the *Acts*, &c. about their keeping Sabbath, I think any Man may reasonably suppose, that *Paul* who kept every Sabbath as before, had kept the Sabbath, *Acts* 20. 7. And that when the Seventh day was over, *Paul* and the Disciples met that Evening (that is, the Evening of the First day) being ready to depart on the Morning (which Evening his readiness to depart on the morrow seems to imply) which the Doctor p. 31. thinks a pleasant shift, which seems a plain and true Fact, for *Paul* there continued his Speech till mid-night, ver. 7, 8. *And when he had recovered* Eutichus, *and broken bread, and eaten, and tarried a long while, till break of day*, Paul *did depart accordingly*, Acts 20. 7, 11. And I know none has yet imagined that *Paul* and the Christians kept two Sabbath days in one Week.

So as supposing the Doctor's mid-night-day mistaken, as I think it is, and supposing the First day to begin in the Evening, which I think it did, and does.

And supposing *Paul*'s manner was to preach every Sabbath in the Synagogue, *Acts* 13. 14, 42. *Acts* 16. 30. *Acts* 18. 4. which he certainly did; and supposing that *Paul*'s preaching in the Synagogue did comprehend his conscientious observing the whole Sabbath day, then instead of a President for the first Day, as the Doctor would make it, putting all those places in the *Acts* together, it seems a President for keeping the Seventh-day Sabbath; and the breaking Bread, and *Paul*'s preaching to the Disciples there that Evening till mid-night, to be both

both after the Sabbath kept and ended, and his travelling the next Morning, *Acts* 20. 11. if it were, as it seems, the Morning of the First day after the Sabbath was over, makes it, that he did not keep the First day, but travelled upon it. So supposing as before the breaking of Bread, imports the Lords Supper, which the Disciples came together for, upon the First day of the Week, that might very well succeed *Paul*'s and their keeping the Sabbath before, upon the Evening of which First day the Converted might come together to receive the Lords Supper together, when they were distinguished from the rest of the Assembly (as is usual in our Assemblys to this day) to whom *Paul* preached Christ upon the Sabbath day before, and departed in the Morning, read and judge, and this is the clear Evidence, which the Doctor says he has from *Acts* 20. 7.

And the Doctor thinks I am not in earnest, and calls it trifling and shifting, (which are hard Words) to render μία σαββάτων, one day of the Week, from which I see no inconvenience when he renders it, אחד, one, which signifies one, yet was the First day, *Gen.* 1. 5. and when he himself renders μία, one, p. 42. and when it is agreed, that tho' μία properly signifies one, which no Grammarian can deny, yet that one was the First day, and so by μία σαββάτων, *Acts* 20. 7. I think may be meant the First day of the Week, tho' the *Greek* εἷς, μία, ἕν, one, be rendred one Scores of times in the New-Testament.

I pass by the Doctor's case of a Horse bought for five Pounds, and paid by five Pounds of Candles, &c. because I have no mind to that way of arguing, by telling old Tales; p. 32. he goes over again the case of the Passover, the days of Crucifixion, and Resurrection, and *Acts* 20. 7. to all which before, and p. 33. the case of *Abel, Enoch, Noah,* and *Abraham,* and from thence till *Israel*'s coming out of *Ægypt,* he says, *I bring no other proof for their keeping the Sabbath, but* Exod. 5. 4, 5.

And if he mean that I bring no other Proof, but one Scripture Proof, that seems somewhat hardly meant.

And he may find in the *Enquiry,* and here before, other Proofs besides *Exod.* 5. 4, 5.

But I had thought one plain, full Word of God for *Israel*'s there keeping Sabbath, or for proving any other Truth, or Matter of Fact, had been enough to convince the most Learned, who acknowledge the Divine Authority of the Scriptures, which I hope the Doctor does and I do.

What

What the Doctor would p. 34. teach me, as to better purpose for the Seventh-day-Sabbath, from *Pharaoh's* seven fat and lean Kine, and the seven days before *Noah's* Flood, and *Nebuchadnezzar's* being seven Years at Grass, and from the three Intervals of seven days, one about the Rain before the Flood, *Gen.* 7. 4. and the other two of *Noah's* staying seven days, and then again seven days before he sent out the Dove, *Gen.* 8. 10, 12. which he says is better Argument then any I bring.

I hope he will not oblige me or any other to believe he so thinks, for if those his Arguments be better then any I bring, I doubt he would not have writ this Book at his Age to Answer them.

P. 34, 35. he says, *There is nothing of a weekly Sabbath in* Job, *which if it were true, needs not, if there be, as there is enough for it elsewhere, in the Word.*

And if you will allow a little Digression, see *Job* 31. 26, 27, 28. which the Doctor p. 64. says, *may perhaps be* Job's *disclaimer of Sun-Worship, which is somewhat towards it.*

And see that of *Eliphaz, Job* 22. 17, 22. *Receive I pray thee, the law at his mouth,* that is Gods Mouth, where the word Law, is the same *Hebrew* Word used *Exod.* 16. 28. about the Sabbath, and *Job* 22. 22. *Lay up his words in thine heart,* so as whenever, and where-ever *Job* lived, tis certain, he and his Friends had some knowledge of the Law, and Words of God, and if of the Law and Words of God, why not of the Sabbath which is his Word, and a part of his Law: See also *Job* 1. 1, 5, 6, 8, 9. *Job* 2. 1, 3. especially *Job* 1. 6. and *Job* 2. 1. which day, at least some of the *Hebrew Rabbies* thought to be the Sabbath.

And although the Doctor p. 35. would make all that is offered in the *Enquiry,* that the Ascension of Christ might be upon the Sabbath day, *Acts* 1. 2, 3, 4, 5, 6, 7, 8, 9, 12. to be a little matter, and yet serving my turn, I refer the Reader for that to the *Enquiry,* p. 43. to which I add, I do not yet see, but that the Ascension day might be upon the Sabbath day, according to *Acts* 1. 12. for I do not think those words, that *Mount Olivet,* (the place of his Ascension) *is from Jerusalem a sabbath-days journey, Acts* 1. 12. which of old was esteemed about two Miles, are so expressed there by the Holy Spirit, but for some special respect to the Sabbath day, which words of a Sabbath-days journey are no where else so expressed in the Scriptures, that I find, but I take it tis agreed by Geographers, that *Mount Olivet* is about

bout two Miles from *Jerusalem*. In *Exod.* 16. 29. *The Lord giveth you on the sixth day, the bread of two days, abide every man in his place, let no man go out of his place on the seventh day*, that is, that day they were not to go abroad into the Field to gather *Manna*, nor to do any other Work, *Exod.* 20. 10. but they might go to the Holy Convocation, *Lev.* 23. 3. And the Cities of the *Levites* were to reach 2000 Cubits from without the City, East, South, West, North, *Numb.* 35. 5. and in *Josh.* 3. 3, 4. when the Ark was born towards *Jordan*, the People were to go after it, yet there was to be a space between them, and it about 2000 Cubits by measure, and they were not to come nearer to it; what those Cubits in measure did extend to, the Jews could best tell us, who thought it about two Miles, which those in the Camp might travel to the Ark, the place of their Publick Worship upon the Sabbath day, *Enquiry, p.* 43. 44, 45. And it seems to me, that *Acts* 1. 12. is so expressed, to shew that Christ and his Disciples going from *Jerusalem* to *Mount Olivet*, and the Disciples going from thence back again to *Jerusalem*, was no breach of the Sabbath day.

But however this were, I think the main question, which is the true Christian Sabbath is built and established upon many other direct full Scriptures before and after cited, which give no colour for denying.

What the Doctor offers for the Feast of *Pentecost*, *Acts* 2. 1. *p.* 37. as to the day when it was, which he thinks was on the First day of the Week, I know no Word for that, or other Ground but Conjectures, and some uncertain *Romish* Traditions, for what day the Fiftieth day was from the true day on which Christ and his Disciples kept the Passover, *Matth.* 26. 17, 18, 19, 20. I do not yet so certainly know, and the Doctor *p.* 12. agrees, that our Saviour kept his last Passover on one day, and the Jews on another: But the most probable Judgment I can make from *Mat.* 26. 17, 18, 19, 20. from *Acts* 1. 12. and *Acts* 13. *Acts* 16. *Acts* 17. *Acts* 18. 4, *&c.* is, that it might be on the Sabbath day, and this is certain, that when the day of Pentecost was fully come, the Holy Spirit was poured out, *Acts* 2. 1.2. But supposing what the Doctor agrees *p.* 12. that Christ kept it one day, and the Jews on another, I think I can prove by the Word, that Pentecost was on the Seventh-day-Sabbath, and not upon the first day of the Week.

But

But this also about what day it was, not being yet so evident to all, and the Sabbath being, as I think, clearly proved by other Texts, I pass it by at present.

I pretermit divers things to which he recurs, p. 38. and takes up again and again what he had written to before, and then the Doctor adds,

A like place is that of 1 *Cor.* 16. 1, 2.

Now concerning the collection for the Saints, as I have given order to the Churches of Galatia, *even so do ye upon the first day of the week, let every one of you lay by him in store, as God hath prospered him, that there be no gathering when I come.*

What likeness there is between those two places I can see very little of, and that this yields nothing at all for his purpose, any man who will read it twice may easily discern, yet he thinks it is plain from thence, that the First day of the Week was weekly observed, and was wont to be observed, both by the Church of *Corinth*, and by the Churches of *Galatia*, which he thinks Paul supposes, and takes for granted, which are all meer Conjectures where I think μία σαββάτων may well be rendred one day of the Week, without any offence.

To which place I think there is answer, *Enquiry*, p. 58. 59. to which I add,

If the Doctor by the Words was weekly observed, and wont to be observed, mean was weekly, and wont to be observed as a Sabbath, or as a weekly Day of Holy Rest (without which he says nothing).

I reply, that here is not one word of any Sabbath or Rest weekly, or other Rest, or of any Worship or Preaching, or any such thing, not one such word, either at *Corinth* or *Galatia*, or taking it for granted, &c. but the quite contrary, that is, an order that they should every one of them lay by in store for charitable Uses, which does include the casting up their Accompts, how else could they know how God had prospered them, which the Doctor p. 39. says scornfully, is a wise Objection, which seems a true and plain Matter of Fact.

What that order was to the Churches of *Galatia*, he says, that I cannot tell, but leaves out my next words, *unless it were to remember the Poor*; and to what is in the *Enquiry*, p. 58. about an yearly Collection, I add, 2 *Cor.* 9. 1, 2. where he said *Achaia* was ready a year ago, and 2 *Cor.* 8. 10. others were forward a year ago.

But

But admitting that μια here signifies First, here is not one word in this order to keep Holy the First day, nothing of that day as a Sabbath, nothing of Praises, breaking Bread, Praying or Preaching, or of any Worship, or Resting here, but only an order for every one of the Christians there, *to lay by him in store as God had prospered him*, which seems also, when they were asunder, and at home, that there might be no gathering when *Paul* came; and this I should think any who read it (without great prejudice) must needs see and know; so that for the Doctor to say he thinks it plain there, that the First day was weekly observed, and wont to be observed at *Corinth* and *Galatia*, and that *Paul* takes it for granted, and supposeth it, &c. without any word for it, seems all from a strong and willing fancy, and very blameable, as highly imposing on the World.

And in *p.* 38. and 39. he reassumes what he had written to before, which in me, without any great cause that I know, he *p.* 39. calls trifling, and Childs-play, which shews him to be angry, and *p.* 41. says, *It must be great Ignorance, or somewhat worse*, which sort of Language agrees well enough in this Cause to prop it up (instead of Word and Argument) with hard Expressions, and if that will please him I shall easily acknowledge my Ignorance and Weaknesses, which are many and great: but withal, I think a weak and simple Man who has the word and command of God on his side, as I think I certainly have in this case, may contend with the most Learned, for whom otherwise I yield my self much too weak.

Nor do I find in all his Book any reason, much less any reason to believe (as he *p.* 42, &c.) that the First day was then generally observed, or wont to be observed, or at all observed, unless by the Heathens, nor that it was according to Christs direction, because we have no word that I know for either, which word is the highest Reason, and why then does the Doctor top upon others those Words, According to Christ's Direction.

And a like saying of the Doctor's we have *p.* 43. by Christs giving commandments to the Apostles, about things pertaining to the Kingdom of God, *Acts* 1. 2, 3. that we are to presume this in particular, about the observing the First day of the Week, and yet there confesseth what those Commandments were in particular we cannot tell, so we are to presume what he admits we cannot tell, which to me is a new Article in Religion made

for

for this purpose. And upon such Presumptions without one word from Christ that I know, the Doctor's opinion seems built.

P. 41. He considers *Mark* 2. 28. *The Son of Man is Lord also of the Sabbath*, and supposeth by Son of Man, is there meant Christ, and if he suppose it, why then does he there controvert it; which Text shews the Sabbath to be the Lords Day, as ver. 27. *The Sabbath was made for man*, shews it was made for the good of Man, for his Spiritual and Eternal good.

And says, *I can't shew that ever the Jewish Sabbath is called the Lords day*, although he knows if he have read the Enquiry, p. 64, 65, 66, 67. that I there quote divers Scriptures, where the Lords Seventh day is called the Lords Day, whereof more by and by, upon *Rev.* 1. 10.

What he says *p.* 43. that I cannot tell whether of the two (that is the Seventh or the First day) is the Seventh day of the Week, does again overturn all his Book, for if it be as he says, uncertain, so as we know not which day is which, how can any Man observe his day in Faith, and what is not of Faith is Sin, and what then is become of all his Arguments for an uncertain weekly First day?

But I think we can tell which is the Seventh-day-Sabbath, and I say as before, from *Nehe.* 9. 13, 14. that *the Lord made known to them his Sabbaths*, his Sabbaths, so the Sabbath was the Lords Day, which they knew; and from him and them we have his Sabbaths. And *Rom.* 3. 2. *to the Jews were committed the words of God*, which with the Old Testament, and therein the Ten Commands they still have; and I think we ought to believe what the Lord Christ accounted and named to be the Sabbath day, was then, and I think is now his Sabbath-day, that is, the Lords Day, *Mark* 2. 28.

P. 44. 45, 46. *Rev.* 1. 10. *I was in the Spirit on the Lords day*, which he would have to be on the First day, which I think I have shewn by the Scriptures, Enquiry, from p. 64 to 68. to be the Seventh day, to which I do not remember he offers any answer (unless some Traditions) to which, to avoid Tautologies, I refer the Reader, and am of the same opinion as there, and without Prejudice, which he would often insinuate, I think, the Lords Day, *Rev.* 1. 10. was not only the name of a day, but the name of the Seventh-day-Sabbath, *Gen.* 2. 2, 3, 4. *Exod.* 20. 10. *Deut.* 5. 14. *Isaiah* 58. 13. *Matth.* 12. 8. *Mark.* 2. 28. *Luke* 6. 5. which Scriptures he that will examine and consider, may easily see that the Seventh-day-Sabbath is the Lords Day, (if the Scriptures be as they ought to be, the rule of judging in this case) which the Doctor would fain have to be the First day, and cannot tell us which day of the Week, the First day is now from Christs time as before, and does not know it, and thinks it impossible to know it.

And p. 46. 47. he again admits, *That Christ was the God who gave the Commandments*, by which he does admit, *that the seventh day there given by Christ is the Lords day*, for Exod. 20. 10. *the seventh day is the sabbath of the Lord thy God*, (i. e.) the Seventh day is the Lords day. And so it often falls out in this debate, that what he and others are constrained to admit in one point, answers what they would deny in another, as I think this does; for if the Lord gave the Commandments, as he did, and as the Doctor admits (together with the Father and Holy Spirit) then he gave the Fourth Command, and therein the Seventh day, Exod. 20. 10. which Seventh day is there expresly said to be the Sabbath of the Lord thy God, that is, to be the Lords day, which as I think by his own admission, tells us, which is the Lords day, Rev. 1. 10.

Of his Traditions, p. 48. 49. (on which the Doctor before) I think there is or can be no certainty from them.

And their Authority to alter any thing in Doctrinals or Practicals, stated in the Scriptures is of no force with me, nor with any Protestant that I know, nor I hope with him, and he may see in the *Enquiry* divers Traditions, Histories, and Records for the Seventh-day-Sabbath, which the Doctor answers not, although I build all upon the Scriptures, and not on Traditions.

I say as before, that Christs manner was not to keep A, but The Sabbath during his Life, and the Women, and others kept it, whilst his Body rested in the Grave, whilst he was in Paradice, that is, in Heaven; not only on what they called the Sabbath, as the Doctor p. 50. which I think not well surmised by him (as if they, or rather the Holy Spirit there called a wrong day the Sabbath) but on what was the Sabbath, and that some of the Disciples travelled upon the very Resurrection day, and that *Paul* and other Christians did not only seem to (which are the Doctor's words, and I think are hard words) but expresly and actually did observe, not only what they called the Sabbath, but what was the Sabbath, the true Seventh day-Sabbath (not only) after Christs Resurrection, but after his Ascension,

sion, and after the Holy Spirit given, and that that was *Paul's* manner, and of others every Sabbath day as before, these Repetitions I am forced to.

Which I think, do prove that Christ and the Apostles did then take not A, but The Seventh day to be the Christian Sabbath (as it was); or why else doth the Holy Spirit so very often in the four Evangelists, before his Death and Resurrection, and in the *Acts* after his Resurrection and Ascension, and after the pouring out the Holy Spirit, name it not A, but The Sabbath, not only what they called, but what was the Sabbath.

Yet the Doctor *p.* 51. thinks *Paul's* Preaching upon the Sabbath days to be occasional, by which, if he means as it there seems occasional only, I know no word he has from God in the Scriptures, for his Sence of occasional, and I think *Paul's* constant Practice to Preach upon the Sabbath days, was according to the Duty of a Minister of Christ, and in Obedience to Christs express Command, *Matth.* 28. 19, 20. by which Command I think all other his Ministers are obliged.

And as to the Passover, and all Sacrifices, and other Ceremonials, that they are abolished by the Death of Christ, I think certain, and to what is said in the *Enquiry*, as to that, I add this,

That the Passover, sacrifices are all set aside by that word, *Luke* 22. 19. and 1 *Cor.* 11. 23, 24, 25, 26. *This do in remembrance of me*, and so the Passover, &c. are laid aside by the Lords Supper, by which Ordinance of the Supper, we declare that Christ was sacrificed for the Sins of his People, and by this we declare his Death till he come in Glory, to judge the Quick and Dead; and there was, or is no further need of Sacrifices, or Types to represent Christs Death. And so the Passover, and all other Sacrifices to be at an end, by these words, *This is my body which is given for you, or which is broken for you, this do in remembrance of me*. Which Lords Supper was then instituted, and immediately succeeded the Passover, which Passover then ceased, *Matth.* 26. 17, 20, 26. *And as they were eating, Jesus took bread*, &c. *Mark* 14. 22, &c.

And to what is offered *p.* 54. from *Rom.* 14. 4, 5, 6. *He that regardeth a day, regardeth it to the Lord, and he that regardeth not the day to the Lord, he doth not regard it*.

G Is

It is not said what was the day there in question, but the Doctor thinks it most likely to be that of the Jewish Sabbath.

What day this was, is hard for any Man at this distance of time to determine, and more hard to build any certain Doctrine upon it, as a certain Day, when God has not that I know, told us in his Word what day it was, but left it wholly uncertain.

I find nothing in that Epistle about days, till *Rom.* 14. 4, 5, 6. where one Man esteemed one Day before another, another esteemed every day, *he that regardeth the day, regardeth it to the Lord, and he that regardeth not the day to the Lord, he doth not regard it.*

And it is not there said (as the Doctor acknowledges *p.* 54.) what was the Day there, nor do I now see how possibly to know what Weekly, or Monthly, or Yearly, or Feasting, or Fasting, or other day it did refer to, but of the Sabbath there is no mention, and why is it then most likely to be the Sabbath, which he confesses is not there said, and whatever day it was, it seems it was no great matter whether they regarded it or not, *ver.* 6.

And whatever day that were, it was certainly such a day as *Paul* would not have them judge one another for, *ver.* 4. which makes it likely to me, that it was not the Sabbath day which *Paul* so constantly preached Christ upon, and observed as before, which Sabbath is a part of that Moral Law which *Paul* was under to God, but was such a day (whatever day it was) as he thought fit at that time and place to leave undetermined.

As for **Gal.** 4. 3, 8, 9, 10.

In Galatia *were some Disciples,* Acts 18. 1, 4, 23. In which Chapter it is said, *Paul preached at* Corinth *every sabbath, to Jews and Gentiles.*

And *Paul,* Gal. 1. 2. directs that Epistle to the Churches of *Galatia,* where probably were some converted, and many unconverted.

And *Gal.* 4. 3. Paul says, *When we were children, we were in bondage under the Elements, or under the Rudiments of the world,* which seems the Heathen World, *ver.* 8. *When they knew not God, they did service to them, who they knew by nature were no Gods,* which was the case of the Heathens, for the *Israelites* did then,

and

and do still Worship Jehovah, who is God, the true God, and so do actually Worship Christ the only Messiah, who is Jehovah, as in the *Enquiry*, p. 9, &c. *And the Father, Son, and Holy Spirit are one Jehovah*, Deut. 6. 4, 5. Enquiry p. 12. *But the Israelites don't yet know Christ to be Jehovah, their Messiah, Saviour, and Redeemer*; which Truth upon their Conversion and Restoration, remains to be revealed to them.

So as this place seems specially directed to those who had an Heathenish Education, who before served those who were no Gods, who after they knew God, Gal. 4. 9. *were turning again to the weak and beggarly Rudiments*, to their first Teachings, and Heathenish Instruction, which Paul there blames ver. 10. *you observe days, and months, and times, and years*, ver. 11. *I am afraid of you, least I have bestowed upon you labour in vain.*

What days these were is the Question, the Doctor says tis not here said in particular, what those days were that are here meant, yet he thinks it is most likely, and scarce to be doubted, to be meant of the Sabbath.

To which I answer, That I think days there cannot be meant of a weekly Rest, and if it be, it is directed there not to rest upon Sunday, which was observed by the Heathens in honour of the Sun, as we may see afterward.

And every Sabbath being observed by *Paul*, and the Sabbath not being (that I can find) in question, days there I think cannot refer to the Sabbath.

Which the Doctor thinks most likely to be meant of the Sabbath, though he acknowledges it is not said; and if it be not so said, how can any mans Conscience build upon what is not said in the Word, and the Heathens generally observed Sunday, and their Princes and Magistrates being Heathens, some of those converted to the Christian Faith, might in some sort decline giving them offence upon their days, whether Feastivals or Fasting days, but that tho it might be is conjectural. 'Tis certain that many do things now which relate to Worship, in complyance with those under whom they live, and so have done I doubt in former Ages, and tis certain they observed days, which observation *Paul* blamed, and some of those days might also be Jewish days, as Passover, New Moons, &c. as in the *Enquiry*, or *days of purim*, Hester 9. 26. which the Jews observe still, as I think, in all Nations where they live.

And

And 'tis to me most likely, and scarce to be doubted, that one of those days blamed by *Paul*, and the principal one was Sunday, which the Heathens observed, wherein the converted Heathens were by their Heathen Parents who knew not God, first instructed before they knew God, *Gal.* 4. 8. which *Paul* calls weak, and beggarly Elements, *ver.* 9. which words of weak and Beggarly Elements do certainly not refer to any part of the Moral Law, as afterward.

So that upon the whole of this in *Gal.* 4. 9, 10, 11. it seems more likely, that *Paul* blames them for observing the First day, if it were at all then observed by Christians.

And *Gal.* 4. 12. which is the next verse, *Paul* adds, *Brethren, I beseech you to be as I am*, who constantly observed the Sabbath day as before.

As to what is objected from *Coloss.* 2. 16. where *Paul* says, *Let no man judge you, in meat or in drink, or in respect of an holy day, or of the new moon, or of the Sabbaths, Greek,* σαββάτων, which the Doctor p. 55, 56, 57, 58. understands of Sabbaths, and so of the Seventh-day Sabbath, and p. 59. does not think it by the Fourth Command to be so determined to this day, that is, the Seventh day, as to be unchangeable to after Ages: And when Christ, or his Apostles by direction from him did put it into a new order; this new order doth as well suit the words of the Fourth Command as that former, all which are *postulata*, and I reply, if it be not changed, then the Doctor cannot change it; and if it be settled in the Word, that the Seventh day is the Sabbath, as I think it is, then it is unchangeable; and the Doctor cannot suit the Command to his Sense, and when the Doctor (or any other) produceth any such new order from Christ, or from his Apostles to change the Seventh to the First day, he will say somewhat, and I hope all Christians will obey it, but I see not yet any such new order produced.

In the General, I acknowledge this of *Coloss.* 2: 16. at first seemed the most colourable Objection that I knew.

Colosse is said to be in *Phrygia*, and the Inhabitants Heathens, this Epistle *Coloss.* 1. 1, 2. *Paul* directs to the Saints, and faithful Brethren in Christ, which are at *Colosse*, which it seems were converted Heathens, and it may be some persecuted and converted Jews, *ver.* 9. 10. *Paul* prays for them, *that they may be fruitful in every good work, of which good work the law of God is a rule*, and *ver.* 13, 14, 15, 16. *Paul* tells them, *that the son of God the redeemer,*

deemer created all things, whom *ver. 5. he* calls the *Lord Jesus Christ, to whom those who were enemies by wicked works* (which wicked Works I think were Works against the Moral Law) *were then reconciled to present them*, ver. 22. *holy, and unblameable, and unreproveable in his sight*, (free from all *Immoralities*) *and present them perfect in Christ Jesus, whom as they had received, so they should walk in him*, which good Works Perfection, receiving Christ, and holy Walking, I think were true Conversion, sincere Repentance, Faith, Holiness, and new Obedience to the Word of God and Moral Law.

And *Coloss.* 2. 8. *Beware least any man spoil you, through Philosophy, and vain deceit, after the tradition of men, after the rudiments of the World, and not after Christ.*

The Philosophers (who are thought to have been Platonists) would then, as others now, have brought the Doctrine of Christ, and Laws of his Kingdom, to be judged by their Reason, who were Heathens, who would have put a cheat upon them by their Traditions, to withdraw them from Christs institutions, after the Rudiments, or first Teachings of the Heathenish World, which were corrupt.

The Heathens had other Objects, (as Sun, Moon, and Stars, &c.) and ways of Worship, contrary to Christ and his Laws.

Let no man therefore judge you in meat, or in drink, or in respect of an holy day, or of the new moon, or of the sabbaths (or *weeks*) Coloss. 2. 16.

Let no man judge or censure you, or impose upon you, that as necessary, which is not after Christ and his Laws; there were Festivals among the Jews which were Typical and Ceremonial, and amongst the Heathens which were Idolatrous.

Against which Rudiments of the World, *ver.* 8. *Paul* speaks more from *ver.* 20. to 23. to which *Paul* would have them dead, and not as tho living in the World, (which was there Heathenish) to be subject to Ordinances after the Commandments and Doctrines of Men (of Heathenish Men) which things have indeed a shew of Wisdom in Will-Worship.

Which second Chapter seems mainly aimed against the Philosophical Heathenish World, and their Will-Worship, after the Commandments and Doctrines of Heathenish Men.

Though

Though some Learned Men have also thought, that it refers to the Inclinations of some there to the Ceremonial Laws, abolished by the Death of Christ.

Now that the Greek word σαββάτων, Sabbaths, does signifie Week, or Weeks, I refer to the *Enquiry*, p. 70, 71, 72, 73. *John* 20. 1, 19. μία τῶν σαββάτων, *Luke* 24. 1. the like 16. 2. σαββάτων, *Matth.* 28. 1. σαββάτων, which in the plural number doth signify Sabbaths, or Weeks, and in the New Testament is used for Week, and for Sabbath, whether it be put there for Weeks I cannot now examine, nor do I see it necessary, seeing the plural number does ordinarily signifie more then one.

What I offered in the *Enquiry*, p. 70. that the word Sabbaths in the New Testament is never applyed to the weekly Seventh-day-Sabbath, was mistaken by me, and the word never, should have been left out, or the Expression otherways cured; and *Enquiry* p. 136. that God who reserved a Tenth of our Substance, reserved, But, a Seventh of our Time, But, should have been left out.

Both which, with other Errata's before, I read it in any Printed Book, I gave particular order to amend, in a Printed Paper of Errata's, and upon a question which requires such variety, by so old and weak a Man as I am, besides Errors in Transcribing, and Printing under some Difficulties, it will be strange if there be not now committed more and greater Errors, which a little Candour and Temper would easily excuse.

And p. 45. the Doctor takes a third exception, and writes near half a page upon it, on a similitude I use of *Moses, no man knows of his Sepulchre to this day*, that is, no Man ever knew where his Sepulchre was.

And as to the Similitude or Comparison referring to the day of Christs Incarnation, the Doctor would rather say, at this day then (as I) to this day, which great Exception can hardly be excused, for in that similitude I think he mistakes my words, and meaning also.

At the Incarnation some then knew the day tho no Man At this day knows what day it was, and the Doctor agrees the day of the Week, or Year, of Christs Incarnation is now not known so as this Exception of to, against at, seems very little at best.

And

And I think he knows that the Lord buried *Moses* in a Sepulchre unknown, not only at that time, but to this day, *Deut.* 34. 6.

Now tis true the Greek word Sabbath, in the plural number, in the New Testament is also applyed to the Sabbath, as to the Week, *Matth.* 12. 15, 10, 12. σαββάτῳ, and 28. 1. σαββάτων, &c.

So that σαββάτων, the plural number, (from the Greek word, σαββάτον, a Sabbath, in the singular number) is in the New Testament sometimes understood of the Sabbath, and sometimes of the Week, and in *Matth.* 28. 1. properly meant of both.

And so the question remains, Whether Sabbaths *Colossians* 2. 16. ought to be rendred Sabbaths, or Sabbath, or Weeks; and if Sabbaths, Whether the Seventh day be there meant, or no?

The Doctor thinks Sabbaths here must be meant of the Seventh-day-Sabbaths (which words, must be one very positive, and against the Opinion of many Learned, as by and by) which he thinks it manifest, *p.* 56. *were there in dispute*, (which dispute I cannot find in that Epistle, nor any where else in the Word) and why then does the Doctor without the Word think it to be there in dispute, and manifest? and he thinks it was then at an End, (which End we read not in the Word) but find it still observed in many Churches of Christ to this day, *Enquiry, p.* 106. to 112, 118, 119, 120.) and why then does he think it was then at an end.

Nor do I find any new order from Christ or his Apostles, as he surmises, *p.* 59.

And if Sabbaths, *Coloss.* 2. 16. do mean Weeks, and not the Weekly Sabbath day, then that Objection of the Doctor falls, and if it mean the First day (*i. e.*) Sunday, which the Heathens observed, then it is against the Doctor so far as *Paul's* blaming their judging will go.

And if it mean Weeks, as it seems to me more likely it ought to be here rendred, or if it means Ceremonial Sabbaths, then so far as this reaches it refers to the Observation of Weeks, and Ceremonial Sabbaths now abolished.

But both one and other seem to me uncertain now, to build any (must be's) upon.

And

And *Coloss.* 2. 16. *Let no man judge you in respect of a feastival, or of the new moon, or of the sabbaths.* Beside the Seventh-day-Sabbath, there were at least three Feastivals or Sabbaths amongst the Jews.

At the Passover, the Feast of Unleavened Bread seven Days, from which Passover, *Lev.* 23. 4, 5. we have the pretence for *Easther,* now ceased as before.

The Feast of *Pentecost,* fifty days after the Passover, that is, seven Weeks after, *ver.* 15. 16. where we have the pretence for *Whitsuntide.*

There were also the Sabbaths of Years, *every seventh year shall be a sabbath of rest unto the Land, a sabbath for the Lord,* Lev. 25. 4. *And after seven sabbaths of years,* ver. 8. *they were to sound the trumpet of the Jubilee,* ver. 9. *and ye shall hallow, or sanctifie the fiftieth year,* ver. 10. And hence (as I take it) we have the ground of the *Roman* Jubilees.

Now it seems to me, that if the word there do mean Sabbaths, that those three may be blotted out, and taken out of the way, and all Heathenish Feasts, Feastivals, Weeks, and Sabbaths, as well Sunday as the rest, *Coloss.* 2. 14.

But that which I think does fairly and fully answer the whole Objection from *Coloss.* 2. 16. besides what is hereafter offered by Learned Men, may be, that this is a caution against judging the Believers at *Colosse,* in *meat, or in drink, or in respect of the Feastivals, new moons, or sabbaths,* and seems to agree with Rom. 14. 4, 5, 6. *Who art thou that judgest another mans servant, one man esteemeth one day above another, another esteemeth every day,* and at *Rome* and *Colosse,* were then cautious against judging the Christians about days.

And we find not in either of those Epistles one word to alter the Seventh day to the First, or to institute the First, all that would be a forced interpretation, the Text is against judging of Christians there about days.

And whether it be meant at that time and place, of judging for or against those Meats and Drinks, or Days or Feasts, or Fasts, or Weeks, or Sabbaths, whatever they were is not now over easie to be resolved.

'Tis likely some converted Teachers, whether Jews or Gentiles, I know not, had taught what was not right about Days, which *Paul* here corrects.

And

And tis certain there are some things in *Paul's* Epistles hard to be understood, 2 *Pet.* 3. 16. and if they were hard to be understood in *Peter's* time, which was *Paul's* time, for they were Contemporaries, much more hard now near 1700 Years after; and by whom hard places in *Paul's* Epistles were then wrested, we may gather a little light, 2 *Pet.* 3. 17. αθεσμων, such as were not subject to the Law of God, were the wresters, and this place in *Col.* 2. 16. seems strongly wrested beyond the words of it, which are against judging the Saints at *Colosse*, in those respects at that time, when the *Ministers of the Gospel had much to do to preach Christ, and by Christ to lay the foundations of christianity, which foundation in the Lord Jesus Christ, the Redeemer and Creator of all things,* Paul *soundly laid in this Epistle,* Coloss. 2. 3, 14, 16.

Which Caution against judging one another, was, no doubt, at that time and place necessary, and rightly understood, is still of great use.

And *let no man beguile you, or seduce you,* Coloss. 2. 17. *Wherefore, if ye be dead with Christ from the Rudiments of the world, whether Heathenish, or Jewish, Why are ye subject to Ordinances,* ver. 18. *which are nothing else, if not instituted by Christ, or if laid aside by him, but human inventions,* ver. 20. *according to the commandments and doctrines of men,* ver. 22. *which are appointed, not by the Lord, but according to the pleasure of men,* as I think the First day is, whereas the Seventh day is appointed by the Lord, and *the Conscience and whole life of man, ought to be governed by the commandments of God, without adding or diminishing,* Deut. 12. 32. Matth. 15. 6, 9.

Which commandments of men, have indeed a shew of wisdom in will-worship, Coloss. 2. 23. Worship which some men imposed on themselves and others, as if they could do and teach better and wiser then God had commanded, which it seems is an old and humane Infirmity.

Mr. *Cawdrey,* and Mr. *Palmer,* in their Treatise of the Sabbath, pag. 50. say, *That the Apostle in* Col. 2. 16. *speaks of the other Holy days and Sabbaths, and not of the weekly Sabbath.*

Mr. *Sheppard* in his Doctrine of the Sabbath, pag. 166. Thes. 181. speaking of Gal. 4. 10. Rom. 14. 4, 5. Col. 2. 16, &c. saith, *If we suppose that these places be meant of the weekly Sabbath, and riggidly urge them, we may quickly press Blood instead of Milk out of them, and wholly abolish (as* Walleus) *the Observation of any Christian Sabbath.*

Doctor *Owen*, in his Treatise of the Sabbath, *pag.* 214. speaking of *Col.* 2. 16, 17. saith, *It is known, and confessed, that at that time all judaical Observations of Days, whether Feasts, or Fasts, Weekly, Monthly, or Annual, were by themselves and all others called their Sabbaths.* And that kind of speech which was then in common use is here observed by our Apostles, *it must therefore necessarily be allowed, that there were two sorts of Sabbaths amongst them, the first and Principal was the Weekly Sabbath, so called from the rest of God upon the finishing of his Works, and that other day became from their Analogy, thereto to be called Sabbaths also.* But that the difference between these Sabbaths was great, *The one of them was ordained from the foundation of the world,* before the entrance of Sin, and so *belonged to all mankind in general* (to all Mankind) the other were appointed in the Wilderness as a part of the peculiar Church-worship of the *Israelites*.

That the one was directly commanded *in the Decalogue,* wherein *the Law of our creation* (the Learned Doctor calls it the Law of our Creation) *was revived and expressed,* and that the other have their Institution expresly among the residue of ceremonial temporary Ordinances. See to the like purpose, p. 215, 216, 217.

Mr. *Richard Byfield*, in his Treatise on the Sabbath, *p.* 130. on *Col.* 2. 16. saith, *That the Apostle there speaketh not of the Fourth Commandment, because he treateth expresly of those Sabbaths which were of the same rank with the New Moons.* And that he speaketh as he doth to the *Galatians, chap.* 4. 10. *of the Observation of Days, Months, and Years, which pertained to the Servitude and Bondage of weak and beggarly Rudiments,* as in *ver.* 9. Now (saith he) *that any precept of the Decalogue should be so accounted, and reckoned as a weak and beggarly Rudiment, was far from the Apostle to think, and is abhorred to Christian Ears, and Religion.* Which I think Answer to the Doctor's Objections from *Col.* 2. 16, &c.

Which four Opinons I had from another hand since I came to *London*, and if I had the use of my own persecuted Study, and other Books here, 'twere easie I think, to gather many more.

And upon the whole, I find *Col.* 2. 16. to be against judging of Christians then and there, and for ought appears against judging either way, and so this place, in whatsoever sence we take it, makes only against judging in those cases.

Pag.

Pag. 59. the Doctor takes the Law for the Seventh-day Sabbath to be a new Yoke to the Gentiles, because it was given to the Jews as a Sign, or a distinctive mark, and for a perpetual Covenant, Exod. 31. 13, 16, 17. Ezek. 20. 12, 20. But this also will be against him, as we shall see by and by.

That it was then new to the Heathens who observed Sunday I agree.

Tis true, it was a sign, but such a sign as all Proselytes did embrace and obey, till the coming of Christ, and *by him is made a perpetual law*, Matth. 5. 18, &c. *and so a perpetual sign between him and his people.*

And tho Circumcision were a sign, yet that is ceased, as before, and Baptism instituted.

And the *Pascal Lamb*, tho it were a distinction between the *Israelites, &c.* and the *Ægyptians*, yet being a Type of Christ, was lain aside by him at his Institution of the Lords Supper, as before by the words, *This do in remembrance of me*, Luke 22. 19. and ceased at his Death.

And if it be meerly circumstantial, and doth not at all influence Religion, whether in the Temple or other place God be Worshipped, *John* 4. 21. as the Doctor, p. 60. & p. 2. Yet God having so directly resolved, that the Seventh day is the Sabbath, that is not a new Yoke, but an old Institution, for the good of all Mankind, *given at the Creation, and commanded in the Decalogue, and so given by Christ.* And with the rest of the Commandments, Matth. 5. 18. and Luke 16. 17. *made perpetual by him*, and so I think is Christs Yoke, and an easie Yoke, (for it is only to take the commanded weekly Seventh instead of the First day.) Matth. 11. 29, 30. which the Doctor and others should willingly take upon them.

Pag. 60. he adds, *That the Jewish Sabbath* (so he often calls it, and the Word Jewish runs much in his mind) *seems to be, not a continuation of a former Sabbath, but rather a new Institution* (which I cannot find in the Word) as he says he has shewed before, which upon all the search I have made, I cannot find in all his Book; and I am loath to observe what I often read therein, the great Latitude he takes that way.

H 2 The

The Doctor p. 69. quotes the *Enquiry*, p. 26. and says, *I press and put great weight upon it, that the Seventh day is a Sign and perpetual Covenant, to distinguish his People from others, that is,* saith he, *the People of the Jews from other Nations*; which last words, *the People of the Jews from other Nations*, are added by the Doctor, whereas my words and meaning was, and is throughout, that the Sabbath was and is a perpetual Sign and Covenant with all true *Israelites*, that is, all true Believers of all Nations, in all Ages, from the beginning of the World to the end of it, to distinguish such from the disobedient to Gods Laws.

And such Artifice to add somewhat of his own to turn what is offered into his own Notion are blameable.

And for the Doctor to say, as he there, *That Circumcision, the Passover, and the Seventh-day-Sabbath, were distinctive Marks, and at an end by the Death of Christ*, is not so. 'Tis true of Circumcision and the Passover that they are at an end, as before, but not of the Sabbath.

So that a particular unravelling the many Allegations which I think are not so, would make this Reply too large.

And he there makes the Sabbath abolished.

By which affirmings he may make other Commands abolished, if his Sayings and Comments may pass for Doctrine, to abolish and overthrow any part of the Law of God.

And adds there, *That it is as meerly circumstantial* (as the place of Worship is) *whether a Sabbath be kept on this or another day*, which is the Doctor's Opinion, I think directly against *Gen.* 2. 2, 3. and against the Moral Law, *Exod.* 20. 9, 10, 11. *Established and made perpetual by Christ*, Matth. 5. 17, 18. *Luke* 16. 17. besides his indifferency to this or another day.

My taking notice of the Doctor's Allegations about Facts which much concern this question, may be excused, for that otherways some Readers may take them for true, and so be misled in their judging this Case, and many I have passed by, which observing Readers may note.

Pag. 61. he repeats from *Exod.* 31. 13. that the Sabbath is a Sign, and yet *p.* 60. 61. doubts, was either not observed at all, or long before this time had been forgot.

To which I Reply, if the Sabbath were a Sign, and such a perpetual Sign, to be kept throughout their Generations, as it was (as the Doctor) and if it were a perpetual Covenant between the Lord and them, as it was (as the Doctor) and made known to them as before, then surely they knew what day of the Week it was, and forgot it not, but observed it as they do, everywhere where they live to this day, which the Doctor has no reason that I know to doubt.

And if that were so, that the Sabbath was long before forgot, and if the days of the Week are all uncertain, and none can tell which was which, Where are we then, but in utter uncertainties?

And these Objections from the Seventh-day-Sabbath being abolished, and a perpetual Sign (and yet forgot and uncertain) contradict one another.

Pag. 61. he says, *God had a particular respect to their Rest from their Bondage in Ægypt, by the Preface to all the Commands, I the Lord thy God, which brought thee out of Ægypt, and by the close of this Command, as repeated* Deut. 5. 15.

I Reply, be it so, yet that was such a Deliverance, as the Gentiles then had a share in, and as concerned all the People of God, at that time in the World, to take special notice of, and such a Deliverance as is celebrated by all the Christians in the World to this day, and doubtless will be so by all such to the end of the World, and is celebrated as such I think in the *English* Common-Prayer Book: See their Catechism.

He there again recurs to *Exod.* 16. for a new *Epocha* of days, which is Replyed to before, that I find no such thing there, as a new *Epocha*.

And *pag.* 62. he says, *As God by* Moses *did give a new* Epocha *or Beginning to a Circulation of Sabbaths at* Marah, *so might Christ by himself, or his Apostles, fix another* Epocha *from his Resurrection.*

I Reply, that neither of these *Epocha's* being found in the Word, I think the Doctor blameable for saying God did give a new *Epocha* by *Moses*, which we do not read he did give, and if it be not in the Word, Why does the Doctor affirm, that God by *Moses* gave it?

And

And he says, *It is not expresly said that Christ did bid his Apostles to fix another Epocha from his Resurrection*, yet he says he gave them Commandments for that purpose, Acts 1. 2, 3.

Now for the Greatest Man living to say, Christ gave them Commandments for that purpose, without a word from Christ for that purpose, seems to me highly blameable, *Every word of God is pure, add thou not unto his words, least he reprove thee*, Prov. 30. 5, 6.

We do suppose with Reason, the Commandments given by Christ to the Apostles were *to preach the Gospel, to disciple all Nations, to baptize in the name of the Father, and of the Son, and of the Holy Spirit, and to teach all things he had commanded them*, Matth. 28. 19, 20. And see *Mark* 16. 15, 16, 17, 18. *Luke* 24. 46. to 52, &c.

And we have other Commandments of Christ to some of his Disciples, *John* 21. 1, 2. where he gave this to *Peter* (and in *Peter* I think to all the rest, and to all succeeding Ministers of Christ) ver. 15. *feed my Lambs*, ver. 16, 17. *feed my Sheep*, ver. 19. *follow me*, which things did and do pertain to the Kingdom of God, of which things *Acts* 1. 3. Christ spake, but what Commandments in particular Christ gave to the Apostles for a new *Epocha*, does not appear that I know there, or elsewhere in the Word. But when they are produced, I hope his Ministers and Churches will receive them, and what else the Apostles had by Inspiration of the Holy Spirit, after Christs Ascension, concerning the ordering of his Churches, and rightly constituted Offices, or concerning any thing else which are recorded in the Scriptures, we readily embrace.

And I may request the Doctor to take heed how he grafts any other Commandments for any purpose on Christ, but what are written in his Word, and if there be no such Commandment from Christ in the Word for that purpose, for his Apostles to fix another *Epocha* from his Resurrection; Why does the Doctor affirm it, if his Cause were good? yet such means to defend it I think cannot be justified, and such affirmations in Facts material to the main question, I think ought to be reproved.

As to what is said p. 62. *That not one jott or tittle of the law*, meaning the Decalogue, *is destroyed* (I think he means that in *Matth.* 5. 17, 18.) *but doth still continue in force*, and that we are all under that Law, as to the substance of the Duty.

I Reply, that he there again acknowledges *that we are all under that Law*, that is, under the Ten Commands, and that they still continue in force.

And if so, I would ask the Doctor one Question, who asks me Divers.

Who can resolve us what is, and what is not Substance in Gods Commands, but God himself who gave them? he knows what bad work several have made by endeavouring to mangle them, especially those of the first Table, and indeed those of both Tables.

For what is said p. 62. that *Matth*. 24. 20. *Pray that your flight be not in winter, nor on the sabbath day*, which flight was about thirty eight Years after Christs Resurrection, that that makes nothing at all to my purpose.

I think a fair answer to that is in the *Enquiry*, p. 73. 74. to which I add, that we cannot as well argue from hence, that it were a Sin to Labour in Winter, as on the Sabbath day, as the Doctor, p. 63. for that the Sabbath and Winter stand on different Reasons, which are obvious; the Sabbath was commanded, and the Winter bad to fly in because of the Cold, Wet, &c. and work was not forbidden in Winter, which was forbidden on the Sabbath, as the Doctor knows; and so *Matth*. 24. 20. seems to the purpose, for the Sabbath was to continue by that Text, *after the Death of Christ*.

Pag. 63. my many other little Excursions, as little to the purpose he will not name, which is a short way of answering.

But says I take great pleasure to expose the name of Sunday, by which name for distinction, I sometimes call it, as himself does often, which (if he pleaseth) he may henceforth call the First day; its true name, as I often do, and other snubbing of Sunday (as the Doctor there) I remember none, but he often calls the Lords Sabbath by a reflecting addition, which I often pass by without snubbing again.

He says, *'Tis true, some of the Heathens did Worship the Sun, but that they did it more on Sunday then on Monday, or Tuesday is more then he knows, or I can prove*.

For Reply to which see *Enquiry*, p. 88, 89, 90. And for his, and others satisfaction herein, I refer them to Mr. *Chafies* Learned Tract on the Fourth Command, Reprinted 1692. which Reprinting I think of use, being a Learned and Moderate Tract,

tho

tho I think Mr. *Chafie* is out in the main Question about the Seventh day, but helps much to prove the Worshipping the Sun weekly upon Sundays, and many other Truths.

In which Tract, Mr. *Chafie*, p. 20. chap. 9. does shew, that the *Assyrians* (which seems to have been before *Moses*, and one of the first Heathenish Dominions) and that all Nations Worshipped the Sun, with which Idolatry, he says, the *Ægyptians*, and many of the *Israelites* and generally other Nations were infected, where p. 23. Mr. *Chafie* tells us, *That those Sun-Worshippers, on what Days of the Week they gave especial Worship to the Sun or Moon, those Days were called by the Names of the Day of the Sun, that is Sunday, and the Day of the Moon, that is Monday.*

So as Sunday is a very ancient day of the Week, and by him it appears they did very antiently divide their time by Weeks; which ancient weekly Sun-Worship, I think is proved by the Prohibition, *Deut.* 4. 19. See also *Ezek.* 8. 16. 2 *Kings* 23. 5. *Deut.* 17. 3, &c.

In which 9*th Chap.* of Mr. *Chafie's*, we have also, how the Heathens always Worshipped towards the Sun rising, *pag.* 26. 27, 28, 29. which Authorities the Doctor may easily find.

Mr. *Chafie* says, not any Nation of Note under Heaven, but adored the Sun as their God (the Sun was King, and the Moon was Queen, but the Sun was Trump). The *Chaldeans, Persians, Ægyptians, Phenecians, Trojans, Grecians, Romans, Scythians, Æthiopians, Tartars,* &c. all Worshipped the Sun.

And p. 71. Mr. *Chafie* says, *That Sunday was so called from our Heathen Ancestors, who called this day* (that is Sunday) *so in honour of the Sun, whom they Worshipped upon Sunday.*

And p. 30. Mr. *Chafie* tells us, *That to take off the Israelites from this Idolatry, the Lord used this means for one, that they should not have the day of the Sun* (that is, Sunday) *for the day of his Worship, but the day before,* (that is, the Seventh day) which I think refers to the time of the 16th or 20th of *Exodus,* which proves not only the Observation of the Seventh day by the *Israelites,* but of Sunday by the Heathens, and that very anciently, and that continually in the weekly Circulation of Days, to this day, tho' I think Mr. *Chafie* be out about the change of the Seventh day, as before and after.

And

And Mr. *Chafie chap.* 15. *p.* 59. gives the Testimony of divers Ancient and Learned Writers, which shew that the day of the Sun with the Gentiles was a Week-day, even the same which *Mathematici*, the Mathematicians (of old) called Sunday, which seem sufficient Proofs, that the Sun was Worshipped on Sunday, and that weekly, and that very anciently.

Which 9*th.* and 15*th.* Chapters of Mr. *Chafie,* I think might give satisfaction, that all Nations of Note under Heaven Worshipped the Sun, and that very anciently, as far back at least as the time of *Moses,* and that upon Sunday, and that towards Sunrising, that is, towards the East, and that weekly, whilst the *Israelites* Worshipped weekly towards the West, upon the Seventh day.

And Mr. *Chafie, p.* 32. *chap.* 10. tells us, *That the Holy Place,* (or Holy of Holies) *in the Temple at* Jerusalem *was towards the West, and that when Worshippers Prayed there, and Bowed, their Posteriors were towards the Sun-rising, and their Faces Westward,* and that Temple was built by the Lords special Direction.

Which is one of the means (assigned by Mr. *Chafie*) God used to take off the *Israelites* from Worshipping the Sun, so Sun-Worship was long before that.

Which Tract of Mr. *Chafie,* I shall a little further consider afterward.

Pag. 65, 66, 67. the Doctor considers the Names of our Days, Sunday, Monday, Tuesday, Wednesday, Thursday, Friday, Saturday, which being now the known Names of the Days, he thinks we need no more scruple the use of these Names, then to talk of Pope *Pious, Clement, &c.* Which I think he gives as answer to what is in the *Enquiry, p.* 90. against those Names of Days, whose Original the Doctor agrees to be from Heathenish Idols.

To which I Reply, from one of the Texts quoted in the *Enquiry; Exod.* 23. 13. *Make no mention of the names of other Gods, neither let it be heard out of thy mouth,* which Learned Mr. *Chafie p.* 30. *l.* 25, 26, 27. thinks refers to the Idol Names of the Days of the Week, which also proves the Antiquity of Sunday, and the Antiquity of Weeks. And the changing those Names of Days I remember, was propounded by some of the Reformers, about the beginning of the Reformation in *England:* And Pope *Sylvester,* the first of that Name, hating the Name and Memory of the Gentile Gods, gave order that the Days should be called by the Name of *feriæ*, as I remember they are named in the Centuries.

And it seems to me in this, and some other cases, the main Doubt is, Whether we shall be ruled by the Word or no?

And the Names of our Days of the Week being Idolatrous, as the Doctor agrees; I did in the *Enquiry*, p. 90. upon the occasion of Sunday, say a little about them, upon which the Doctor expatiates, and falls hard upon Scruples.

Now causeless Scruples I yield are a Weakness, but a true Conscientious Tenderness of Mind, not to offend God in any thing, wherein his Will in his Word is made known, is as I think, one of the most excellent Frames in Man. And if the Doctor under his Notion of Scruples, thinks to reflect upon Conscientious Obedience to the Word, or any part thereof, (which I hope he does not) he will be much to blame, and God having so expresly forbidden the mention of the Names of Idols, as these were by which the Days are called Sunsday, Moonsday, Tuiscosday, Wodensday, Thorsday, Frizasday, Saturnsday.

Anp having also expresly given us in his Word, the proper true Names of the first, second, third, fourth, fifth, sixth, and seventh Days, which Seventh day is called the Sabbath throughout the Scriptures, how ever that may seem to the Doctor, I make no Scruple to call the Days of the Week by the same Names as the Lord calls them; and if the Doctor will retain the old Idol Names without Scruple, notwithstanding his own acknowledgement whence they are, and notwithstanding the Word against them, I cannot help it, and it seems to me the most subtile of those, who are so fond of holding fast the Idol Names of Days, do doubt the consequence of laying them aside, as if it might by degrees introduce both true Names and Things.

What is said *p.* 68. 69, 70. (upon the occasion of Scruples) about Spiritual Worship, and Worshipping in Spirit and in Truth, I think does much concern all that fear God. But because he does not speak out directly, but only falls upon Scrupulosities, and Shadows, and Circumstances seemingly, though I think it pretty plain what he reflects upon, I shall reply but a little to that, and do refer the Reader to the *Enquiry*, p. 32. where he may find in few words what I think from the second Command (besides

sides many other Scriptures) of Forms of Worship, Graven, Printed, or Written, and not instituted by the Lord, but invented.

And in Reply to another, I think *Luke* 11. 2. compared with *Matth.* 6. 5, 6, 7, 8, 9. about the Lords Prayer, that the same Cautions of, *into thy Closet, shut thy Door, and in secret, and in secret,* &c. *Matth.* 6. 6. do refer to, and explain *Luke* 11. 2. By which Cautions I think he should be governed, and *Enquiry,* p. 32. he may see what I think from *Eph.* 5. 18, 19. *Col.* 3. 16. about singing; all which, and much more, some may count little things, Scruples, and causeless Scruples, nice Speculations, and needless Scrupulosities, whereby (as such may pretend) men are diverted from the Substantials of serious Religion, and spiritual Worship, which I think are very hard Reflections.

Now I doubt, that not only the *Romish* World, but some others not of that way, as far as I can discern, are yet at some distance from their Duty in those cases, who are held to the Frames wherein they walk by the Authority of Men, and who for years past, have taken a liberty to comply with the Worship of the Country where they live, and take all down without chewing, as they find them, and so I doubt esteem those who differ from them (who upon the most diligent Search, and long Experiance, Worship God as they think, according to the Word) as scrupulous, and as standing for little Circumstances and Shadows, and so Conscientious, Lively, Spiritual Worshipping as but Shadows, and not substance of Christian Worship, and such Worshippers, as diverters of others from serious Religion, many of whose Rods do yet bud and blossom, and bring forth Almonds, which if God so please, I shall be heartily glad to hear of their Rods who reflect upon them.

Which little Circumstances and Shadows as they are called, do not at all, as some pretend, influence the substance of spiritual Worship, but are meer scruples, and minute things; and here it seems we have some thoughts of spiritual Prayer, &c. as before of Preaching. And thus the very Life and Power of Christian Worship is, as I think, reflected upon by some who have Frames of right Worship, 2 *Tim.* 3. 5. and some of them correct Frames, that is, who have a way of Worship which has some similitude, or likeness to right Worship) who change their Glory for that which doth not profit, and drink the Waters of other Rivers instead of Living Fountains, between which seve-

ral

ral Waters there is an internal difference, as great and manifest, as there is between good, wholesome, running and living Springs, and dead Water, which may be some short and weak Reply to the Reflections before mentioned.

And if it were not to avoid offence, I had written, and might write more on this subject, which so much concerns all Mankind certainly, to know how to Worship Jehovah aright, and which for all Mankind, Ministers and others, old and young, who have the Scriptures of the Old and New-Testament, and common Sence, and can speak, and are by Grace made willing, is demonstrably as easie to be put in practice without Crutches, and to be taught even to Children, without more adoe, as for such to be taught, for just Reasons, to speak for any thing they stand in need of, and would desire another, in whose power it is to give unto them.

And upon this occasion I had thought on some Lines about Swearing to a Point, and about abjuring Endeavours, whether lawful, peaceable, and honest Praying and Preaching Endeavours be excluded, but to avoid offence have crossed them out.

And to return: Tho it be all one to the Doctor, whether the days be called Saturday, Sunday, or *Alpha, Beta, Gamma*, in this we differ a little, he takes them as it seems, as he finds them in the World, and I take them as I find them in the Word, and I know no principle amongst men, which does so effectually answer, and cure all blamable scruples, and unquietnesses of Mind, as a sincere Obedience to all the Wills of God, which he that will do shall know, *John* 7. 17. which I doubt taking all as one, finds them, though it may lull in security, will never perform.

Pag. 66. He blames the whole of Judicial Astrology, as precarious, and only a Trick to amuse credulous People, and make a gain of them, which is truly blameable, yet amongst two sorts of People is now very common.

As

As to what is said p. 68. about meeting once upon a Sabbath day, besides Morning and Evening Worship, &c.

I Reply, that I think that most for the real Service of God, and the Good of his People, which God has directed in his Word, which Rule, unless some necessity intervene, will be always found free from all Inconveniences; and for that I refer the Reader to the *Enquiry*, p. 83. 84. Almost all the Questions in these Papers depend much upon this, Whether Man shall be allowed to be wiser then God?

Pag. 69. Whether to begin the Sabbath at Six or Twelve a Clock at Night? he thinks a thing not worth contending about.

And if it be so small a thing, not worth contending about, Why does he not begin it when the Lord began it, that is in the Evening? one would think that none should differ with the Lord over all for a small thing, and of so little worth, when he has in his Word plainly told us his Will.

And tho he thinks it not much more, whether on this, or that day, so the Sabbath be well kept, I do not yet know what he means by well keeping, but the words, this or that day, seem in him very indifferent to either, and I doubt will make any Man of that mind very cold in well keeping it.

I think with the Doctor, we are to avoid foolish Questions, and to study things which make for true Peace, which Gods Word when it is obeyed, does most certainly do, and the foolish Questions are those which cross his Law and Word, and are contrary to it, and striving against his Law and Word, is one of the worst Fruits of the Flesh, which Wars against his Will, and (to use some of his Words) *in whomsoever that Temper is found* (I doubt) *it is for want of true Love, and other Fruits of the Holy Spirit*.

And when some study to spin out Disputes into so fine a Thread as to make the day begin and end at one time, which God has so firmly settled to begin and end at another, Gen. 1. 5, 8, 13, 19, 23, 31. and to make the Week days all uncertain, which is which, &c. is to make that dark and difficult, which the Scriptures and Works of God have made plain.

I think with him, we complain of the *Romanists* (and I think of others also) and deservedly, for loading their Worship with Ceremonies, the number of which (besides that they are meer humane Inventions, and so of no spiritual Use) are a burden which has broken down many eminently Holy and Learned in this Age, and which divert the Mind from Spiritual Worship.

And I think it also somewhat of the same Mischief, when Mens Minds are amused with uncertain dark Speculations, whereby they are endeavoured to be turned away from plain and easie Obedience, and Ground is layen for perpetual Doubts and Scruples, whilst the Word says one thing, and some of great Learning and Influence do and teach another.

And as to the Point in question, I may say (as the Doctor p.70.) *I have upon the whole said, as I weakly can, so much as I think may satisfie others, if they consider it without Prejudice, a temper which the Holy Spirit can give his People, and I know when men have long espoused a Notion by which they have a benefit, which Notion, if they let go, they loose or endanger that benefit.*

It is no great wonder if they go on in their old way, till God does awaken them, but whether they go on with or without Doubts and Scruples, I know not.

Nor do I know any thing can be so plainly said, no, not from direct Word and Law of God, which by an Ingenious and Learned Man, may not be cavilled at, if he be so minded; and God will suffer him, and when the Lord has, as it seems to me, so plainly declared his Will, if some will not submit to it, who else can help it?

And when I have thus said, I leave the Success to the Lord.

Pag. 71. he mentions a late Book on this Subject, to which I had drawn such Answer as I then could, before I saw the Doctor's, but finding, as far as I remember, nothing therein in this case but what is offered with great Advantage by the Doctor, or what may be answered by observing Readers. I think to say but a little more to it.

P. 5. of his Preface, he says, *Suppose the Authors* (he means the Author of the *Enquiry*) *Notion be Orthodox, and the contrary* (that is, his own) *Heterodox, he gives us the pernicious tendencies thereof.*

That

That is, as I understand him, suppose it to be the mind of Christ, and a Sound and Orthodox Opinion, that the Seventh day is the true Christian Sabbath (which is a fair, and I think a true Supposition) yet he is against the Communicating of it as pernicious (which seems to me somewhat harsh) and suppose his own Opinion Erroneous and Heterodox; yet he is for it, and would not, as I understand him, have it contradicted: to which I only Reply, that I doubt the ancient Prophets, the Apostles, and the Reformers from *Rome*, &c. were not of that mind.

In his little Book, he has these and other Reflections on the Author of the *Enquiry*, or on that he there offers, or on those who receive it, &c.

As Judaical, fanciful, baffled, absurd, Heterodox, and impious, scrupulous, superstitious, a Weed, and Thorn, rotten Premises, sandy Foundations, false Measures, Proofs invalid, which it pitties him to see, uncharitable, rigorous, deluded Brain of silly Zealots, impertinency, empty, false Premises, silly Conjectures, against all Reason and common Sense, &c. which seem to me blameable.

And he hopes *p. 56. himself has written by Gods Assistance and Guidance*, and *p. 163. by Gods Assistance*, and *p. 116. by Gods Help,* and (he hopes) *his Guidance*.

Which Expressions I think may be used sometimes, and in some Cases, but men should take heed how they use them, as if they were divinely inspired, when they use them so interwoven.

Pag. 70. to *p.* 79. the Doctor sums up what he has offered, with all the advantages of a Learned Man, (as he sometimes does before) with new words, on which I might make some Remarks.

In that about the Fifth Command, *p.* 82. he tells us, *His Humane Law, that is to determine who is to be reputed the Father*, and this he applys, first to natural Parents, which as cases may be put, may fall very heavy upon many Children, whose Parents were married, but not according to Human Law.

And that General Rule from Humane Law, if I mistake him not, he understands as determining the Law of God, for he says, *p.* 81. *There be many things which the Word of God, or the Divine Law doth determine in* Thesi *(that is in a general Position) which when (in* Hypothesi*) they come in practice, will require the intervention of Prudentials, or Humane Laws*, and he there, and *p.* 82.

puts

puts cases upon the Eighth, Seventh, Sixth, and Fourth Commands.

So his General Rule is applyed to Laws in both Tables.

And what he there says as to Natural Parents, the like he says as to other Superiours, as well as Natural Parents, and those Laws which seem absolute (says he) *have yet their tacit Limitations implyed.*

To which I Reply.

That I think every Man should beware how he sets up Humane Laws, to determine against God's Law in any case, for if Gods Law determine one thing to be a Duty or a Sin, and Mans Law determine the contrary, we are I think to obey God, *Acts* 4. 19. whose Laws are Superiour to all Humane Laws.

And he that in the Duties required in either Table, does allow the intervening, or coming in of Prudentials, or Humane Laws to controul or to determine the Word of God, or the Divine Law, under that colour, or tacit Limitations implyed, and of room for Prudence to interpose, does, I doubt, unlord the Word and Law of God, *Mark* 7. 13. (which unlording the Word, or making it of no effect, *Mark* 7. 13. is also spoken by our Lord there, in the case of the Fifth Command, *v.* 9. to 13.) and does open a gap to enervate that Law of God.

So that for any to say, that his Humane Law that is to determine who is to be reputed my civil Parent, that is, who is my lawful Prince (whatever the Law of God determines in that case) under the subtile Words of *Room*, for Prudence to interpose, and of tacit Limitations implyed, I doubt reserves a liberty inconsistent with the Word and Law of God, and very hard to be defended.

For with those Limitations, and if Humane Laws shall determine the Divine Laws; in some Parts of the World bad Men may find Pretences for the rankest Atheism, Theism, Arrianism, and Blasphemy against the Holy Spirit, notwithstanding the First Command, for the foulest Corruptions and Invasions on Christian instituted Spiritual Worship, notwithstanding the Second, for the highest Prophanations of the Name of the Divine Majesty, notwithstanding the Third, as well as for polluting the Sabbath, notwithstanding the Fourth, and for Rebellion, Murder, Adultery, Stealing, False-witnessing, and Covetting, notwithstanding the other Six. And so it seems to me, such

Limita-

Limitations, &c. have need of many Cautions to correct them.

Now before I answer the Doctor's two Expedients, I first Reply to somewhat more I find in Mr. *Chafie*'s Learned Tract.

Mr. *Chafie* in p. 2. of his Epistle, says, *That Christ the Son of God, hath taken away the Jews Sabbath, and Established another, contrary to what God the Father instituted*, &c.

Now, tho I hope he was a very Good, as well as a Learned Man, yet he seems not to have then had clear Apprehensions of Christ, as creating the World, and then resting, nor of Christ, as instituting the Sabbath, *Gen.* 2. 2, 3. nor of Christ confirming the Moral Law at *Synai*, &c. *Exod.* 20. nor of Christ making it perpetual, in *Matth.* 5. 18. *Luke* 16. 17.

And in that Tract Mr. *Chafie* speaks of one Sabbath at the Creation, another in *Exod.* 16. and another at the Resurrection of Christ; by which Notion he makes (to have been) three Sabbaths, from whom I think the Doctor takes up (if I mistake him not) the like opinion of three Sabbaths, wherein I think they are both out, as before. And hereafter for Mr. *Chafie*'s Notion of one Seventh-day-Sabbath at the Creation, and another Seventh-day Sabbath in *Exod.* 16. I doubt would make two Seventh-day-Sabbaths in one Week of seven Days, which seems to me inconsistent, and would make the First day more uncertain also, besides the uncertainties of the Doctor.

Mr. *Chafie*'s opinion, p. 19, 20. *That God hath not bound men to any set time to begin their Week*; and chap. 8. p. 18. he says, *The Law-giver himself hath plainly pointed out unto us in this Law, that is, in the Fourth Command, which is the Lords Day, or Sabbath of the Lord, and that is the day following the six days of Labour (with Men) and that in every nation, however they begin their Week, the Seventh day thereof is the Lords*, p. 20. l. 9. p. 44. l. 6, 7. and his Epistle, p. 7. l. 4. *and that the Seventh day is not to be reckoned from the six days of God's Labour, but from the six days of Labour with Men*; and so also in his Postscript; but doth acknowledge chap. 11. p. 35. it hath been the general opinion, not only of the Vulgar, but of the Learned also (which opinion of the Learned I think is right) that the Seventh day commanded us in this Law, hath Relation only to the six Work-days of the Lord God, and not to the six Work-days with Men; which opinion of Mr. *Chafie*'s for Mans Day, is, I think, contrary to *Gen.* 2. 2. for *on the seventh day God ended*

ended his work, &c. and rested the seventh-day from all his work; so as twas the six days God wrought, which were the six Working-days, and the Seventh day God rested, when he ended his Work, which was and is the Holy and Blessed Sabbath; which first appointment of the Lord I find no where changed, and so *Exod.* 20. 9, 10, 11. *Six days shalt thou labour, but the seventh day is the sabbath of the Lord, in it thou shalt not do any work,* &c. *For in six days the Lord made Heaven and Earth, and rested the seventh day, wherefore the Lord blessed the sabbath day, and made it holy;* and so it seems very plain, that the six Working-days are those on which the Lord wrought, and the Resting, or Sabbath day, that which the Lord made Holy, and Blessed, and on which he Rested.

And Mr. *Chafie* in *chap.* 12. says, *God by his Law tyeth all Nations, that at what time soever they begin the Week, they work not on the Seventh day, but sanctifie it.*

Which would be true if men began the Week as the Lord directed in *Gen.* 1. but else by that Rule of Mr. *Chafie's,* Friday in *Turkey* (being their weekly Sabbath) the Christians living in *Turkey,* are bound by the Fourth Command to sanctifie Friday, (*i.e*) the sixth Day of the Week, as the Lords Sabbath day, because the *Turks* there so do.

And by the same Rule, those Christians who live in any Heathen Nation, where they Worship the Sun, and observe Sunday, there they must keep Sunday, and Sanctifie it, because the Heathens where they live so do.

And those Christians who live in those Christian Provinces, who keep the Seventh day, must keep the Seventh day as the Lords Day, because others so keep it, and for that reason. And the like of those who live in any part of the World amongst the *Israelites.*

And those Christians who live in those Christian Countries where they keep the Seventh-day-Sabbath, and the First day also, must keep I know not which of them by Mr. *Chafie's* Rule. And I take it as agreed, we are not to keep two Days in a Week, and that there are some such people of these sorts, see *Enquiry,* p. 119, &c.

Which Rule of Mr. *Chafie's,* to resolve which is the Sabbath day commanded by the Practice of the Country where we live, and that God hath not bound men when to begin their Week, is to set up Mans Day, as it seems to me, against the Lords Day,

Day, and I think the Doctor writes by, for he seems to take it as he finds it.

Which Rule I doubt will agree neither with the letter or meaning of *Gen.* 2. 2, 3. or of the Fourth Command.

What Mr. *Chafie* objects, *That by the different Horizons, wherever Paradice was* (which p. 17. he says is unknown) *no man can tell in the place where he liveth, when to begin the Day of Gods resting at the Creation.*

I Answer, if our Sabbath did begin at the same instant of time that Gods first Rest did, and Men were obliged to that instant, then that were an hard objection.

But I know no place in the Word where it is said, that every Sabbath afterward was to begin the same moment or time that the first Sabbath began in Paradice, or at *Synai*, &c. Nor do I remember any thing so offered in any Writer. But that the Sabbath then did, and that Sabbaths afterward were to begin in the Evening everywhere, as Time was distributed into Days at the Creation, I think is before shewn, and that every Day of the Week began in the Evening, and lasted from Evening to Evening, and that the Days began at or about Sun-set, and supposing the Darkness and light were the Evening and Morning of the three first Days; *Gen.* 1. 5, 8, 13. sure the Days then did not begin at mid-night, when Darkness began the Day, and Darkness and Light made up the First day, and so the Second day, and so the Third day, which Word I think may settle that Point, that the Days did not begin at mid-night.

Suppose also the Sun Created, as it was the Fourth day, and went round the Earth every day after it was created, as it did, and does to this Day. But on what part of the Fourth day the Sun was created is not certainly revealed that I know.

The Fowls and the Fishes were created upon the fifth day.

And Adam *was created on the Sixth day, and being created in the image of God, was made capable of knowing and contemplating the Perfections of him that created him, and of observing, and keeping Holy the Seventh day, which presently after his Creation was Consecrated, or made Holy, and Blessed, to let him into that Spiritual and Heavenly Life and Rest, which his State of Innocency made easie and pleasant to him.*

And in Reply to one of the Doctor's Expedients, we may also suppose the Sun when set in the Firmament, *Gen.* 1. 17. travelled Westward round the Earth daily, as it still doth.

K 2　　　　　　　　　　Now

Now when the Sun did set the Fourth day, then the Fifth day began at Paradice, and when the Sun did set there next, the Sixth day began there, and when the Sun did next set there, the Seventh day began there, and that first Seventh day was probably as long as the other Days of the Week were, and are.

And as the Posterity of *Adam* (and so of *Noah*) travelled East, West, North, or South, by degrees the Earth was overspread, *Gen.* 9. 19. and into whatever Country they came, as the Sun did set, so every Day of the Week began, and so on to this day.

I Write as plain as I can.

So as the weekly Seventh day did begin as the Sun did set, in every place round the Earth, from Paradice Westward, till the Sun came about in 24 hours to Paradice again.

And for an instance, and for certainties sake, *I* will begin with the Eleventh of *March*, the vernal *Æquinox*, 169$\frac{2}{7}$. which falls out to be the Seventh day of the Week.

And the Seventh day at the Creation, did begin as the three First days, and the other Week-days did, that is, in the Evening, as Mr. *Chafie*, and many other Learned Men do agree, at, or about Sun set, as I think is before shewn, and lasted 24 Hours, from Evening to Evening, according to *Gen.* 1, and *Gen.* 2.

And the Sabbath day then was as it still is, proportionably as long as the other Six Days of the Week allowed for Work, or rather wherein we are commanded to work, every of which six Days hath a Night or Darkness, as well as Day Light, in which Night or Darkness, if need be, Men may as lawfully work, as in the Day Light, tho generally the Day is made for Work, and the Night for Rest.

And so the Sabbath day hath an Evening, and a Morning, that is, a Night and Day of Holy Rest, in which Night we may take Rest, as in other Nights.

As for those who begin the Sabbath day in the Morning, they lose the Evening, that is, the Night of that Day, which being no part of the Sixth day, nor (to such) any part of the Seventh day, yet 12 Hours of time between the End of the Sixth, and Morning of their Seventh day, would cease to them to be any part of the Week, if their Opinion would hold who begin the Sabbath in the Morning, unless they continue their Sabbath till the next Morning, and so turn God's first Institution upside down.

Others who begin and end the Sabbath day at mid-night, being

ing then generally asleep at both, when they begin and end it, they cannot tell when they begin or end it, and so must needs loose those Meditations which are peculiar to the one and to the other, and how any can begin or end it at mid-night I know not.

But supposing as before, the Evening in all Parts of the Earth, begins and ends the Day, then it is easie for all to know the beginning and ending of it.

And as the Evening and Morning made up every Day of the Week in Paradice, so Evening and Morning, as Mankind came about the Earth, made up every Day of the Week everywhere else, and as the Evening of the Seventh day came, so the Sabbath began, and the Sabbath ended everywhere as the rest of the Days of the Week ended, that is, the Evening after.

And if this be the true Scheme of Days, then somewhere in the Round of the Earth, every Inhabitant of it the 11th. of *March*, 169$\frac{2}{3}$. may not only keep the Sabbath, but certainly know when it begins and ends, and will have also their full six Nights and Days in the Week for their Work and Callings.

And so as *Adam* or his Posterity, and so as *Noah* or his Posterity, travelled into any part of the Earth, East, West, North, or South, where ever they came after six days of Travel, or other Labour, they might, as the Sun did set, Rest the Seventh day.

And all the tying up all parts of the Earth to the precise time or moment of the Lords resting in the Evening of the first Seventh day at the Creation, and that the Seventh day Sabbath everywhere over the Earth, ever after, must begin and end the same minute the first Sabbath began and ended, whether it be at mid-day, or mid-night, or any other part of Night or Day, seems a meer cramping of the Question, without any Ground for it that I know from the Word.

Whereas, if the days begin in the Evening, as I think they do, and if the Evening and the Morning do constitute and make up a day as they do, then all the Scruples raised, when every Day of the Week, and in particular, when the Seventh day-Sabbath, all over the Earth, doth begin, and end, are resolved, that is, in the Evening; and so the two long days in *Joshuah's* and *Ezekiah's* times, make no alteration of Days, as in the *Enquiry*. And so the Evening and the Morning make up every Day of the Week to us in *England*, and to every other Nation

tion in the Earth, and for any other certain way to resolve when the days do begin and end, but by Gods first appointment, I know not, for else it would put the most skilful Mathematicians everywhere to a stand, when to begin and end the Days, and leave all Computations of Days, and Weeks, and Time in uncertainties and great disorder.

I take the 11th. of *March* the vernal Æquinox, because Astronomers agree the Sun to be then in the Æquator, as it is the 11th. of *September*, at the Autumnal Æquinox, at which times, the Days and Nights are by them said to be equal all over the Earth.

And if I had supposed the Sun in his Declination to either of the Topicks, the various Climates, and obliquity of the Horizon, might have occasioned disputes, which, what I can, I avoid, and therefore take the 11th. of *March*, 169$\frac{5}{7}$.

Nor do I enquire the place of Paradice, where it is, about which there are many disputes, which place Learned Mr. *Chafie* confesseth is not known.

And if we know not where Paradice is, then I cannot begin to give Instances of the Scheme before from thence, but if it lies East or West from *Mount Synai*, that will make some difference of time in the beginning and end of Days at *Synai*, and at Paradice, and yet not alter the days of the Week in either, for that the Seventh day of the Week in Paradice, was, is, and will be in the weekly Circulation of days, the Seventh day of the Week there.

And the Seventh day in the Week at *Synai*, though it may differ in degrees of Longitude from Paradice, yet was, is, and will be in the weekly Circulation of Days, the Seventh day of the Week at *Synai*; and so of the rest of the Days there and in every other place, as in Ægypt, *Exod.* 5. 5. where the *Israelites* kept the Sabbath, and *Exod.* 16. 1, 23, to 30. in the Wilderness of Sin.

And yet notwithstanding that difference in Degrees between Paradice and Ægypt, and the Wilderness, and *Synai*, that made no difference between them, as to the beginning or ending of Days.

In Paradice the Seventh day (as the First, Second, and other Week-days) began in the Evening, and ended the next Evening, and so the Seventh day in Ægypt, in the Wilderness, and at *Synai*, began in the Evening, and ended the next Evening. And

at

at all those places, according to appointment at the making of the World, *Gen.* 1. and *Gen.* 2. notwithstanding the different Degrees or Minutes there might be of the Sun-setting at Paradice, and at those places.

The Lord who knows all his own Works, the Beginning or Head of whose Word is Truth, *Gen.* 1. 1. *Psal.* 119. 160. *The entrance of whose words will give light, Psal.* 119. 130. *Blessed and made holy the seventh day Sabbath,* Gen. 2. 3. *at Paradice.*

And *blessed and made holy the seventh day at* Synai, Exod. 20. 11, 12. although it is likely there are some Degrees or Minutes between.

But how ever that be, yet we are pretty certain by the Maps where *Synai* was, and is, and where *Jerusalem* was and is.

And according to the common received Principles of Astronomy, fifteen Degrees making an Hour, *Jerusalem* is situate about six Degrees in Longitude, Westward from *Synai*, and so the Sun sets at *Jerusalem*, after his setting at *Synai*, twenty four Minutes of an Hour, or thereabout, that is, two fifth parts of an Hour, Westward from *Synai*, and yet that difference in the beginning of the Seventh day at *Synai*, and of the Seventh day at *Jerusalem*, made no alteration of the beginning or ending of the Seventh day-Sabbath at either.

The same Seventh day which was commanded to be remembered to be kept Holy at *Mount Synai*, and which was repeated by *Moses* in *Deuteronomy* near *Jordan*, which place near *Jordan* may be about twenty two Minutes of Longitude from *Synai*, was certainly remembered and kept Holy by the *Israelites*, at *Mount Zion* in *Jerusalem*, with this difference, that the Seventh day began at *Jerusalem*, twenty four Minutes of an Hour after it began at *Synai*; and some Minutes after it began near *Jordan*, which made no alteration of Days at either, but the Seventh day at *Synai* began in the Evening, twenty four Minutes of an Hour before it began at *Jerusalem*, and at *Jerusalem*, the Seventh day began twenty four Minutes of an Hour Westward, after it began at *Synai*, and yet was the Seventh day in both, and began in the Evening at both, that is, at or about Sun set at both, notwithstanding the difference in time of twenty four Minutes, which may a little direct how to find when the Seventh day doth begin; and so of the rest of the Days every where.

This may be illustrated by further Instances, and for certainties sake, I will set out, and begin to reckon from *Jerusalem*, where

where they observed the true Seventh day Westward (without setting a Meridian there, altho it be Arbitrary, as the Doctor acknowledgeth, and may be set where we will) and by degrees bring the Account round the Earth to *Jerusalem* again.

From *Jerusalem* to *Colosse*, are about seven Degrees, that is, twenty eight Minutes.

From *Jerusalem* to *Ephesus* 9 Degrees, that is, 36 Minutes.

From *Jerusalem* to *Antioch*, where Paul and his Company kept the Sabbath, Acts 13. 13, 14, 15, 16, 27, 42. &c.

From *Jerusalem* to *Philippi*, now ruined and desolate, which was situated on the confines of *Thrace*, are about 14 Degrees, that is, 56 Minutes, where they kept the Sabbath, Acts 16. 12, 13, 14.

From *Jerusalem* to *Corinth*, are about 17 Degrees, that is, 1 Hour and 8 Minutes, yet this difference of time, and so of beginning of the Sabbath, made no alteration of the Sabbath, where they also kept the Sabbath, Acts 18. 1, 4.

As they did also as *Thessalonica*, Acts 17. 1, 2. where the Sun sets about 1 Hour and 10 Minutes after it sets at *Jerusalem*.

And everywhere as the Sun did set, so the Sabbath day, as every other Day of the Week did begin and end as before.

From *Jerusalem* to *Warsaw* in *Poland*, are about 22 Degrees, that is, 1 Hour and 28 Minutes difference of Sun-setting.

From *Jerusalem* Westward to *Vienna*, are about 29 Degrees, that is, 1 Hour 56 Minutes.

From *Jerusalem* to *Rome*, are about 30 Degrees, that is, 2 Hours.

From *Jerusalem* to *Amsterdam*, are about 40 Degrees (i. e.) 2 Hours and 40 Minutes.

From *Jerusalem* to *Paris*, are 44 Degrees, that is, 2 Hours 56 Minutes.

From *Jerusalem* to *London*, are about 48 Degres, that is, 3 Hours and 12 Minutes.

From *Jerusalem* to *Edinburgh*, 49 Degrees, that is, 3 H. 16 Min.

From *Jerusalem* to *Dublin*, about 53 Degrees, that is, 3 Hours and 32 Minutes.

From *Jerusalem* to *Lisbon*, are about 57 Degrees, that is, 3 Hours and 48 Minutes.

From *Jerusalem* to *New England*, are about 120 Deg. that is, 8 H.

I have passed over the first Meridian (which is Arbitrary as before) and follow the Sun as it goes round the Globe of the Earth, till it comes about to *Jerusalem* again, which as to this way of accounting, I think makes no alteration.

And

And all these differences in Hours and Minutes, from the setting of the Sun at *Jerusalem*, and the setting of the Sun in all these before-mentioned, and all other places in the Earth, make no alteration of the Days, or of the Sabbath, all which begin every where, as the Sun sets every where, and when the Sun every where did set, so the Sabbath day, as every other Day of the Week did begin and end as before.

I still follow the Sun from *Jerusalem* to *Japan*, the Sun may be said to set seventeen Hours at *Japan*, after it sets at *Jerusalem*, and when the Sun sets at *Japan*, then the Seventh day begins at *Japan*, 11 of *March*, 169¾.

And from *Japan* (to pass over the other Meridian, and Rest of the Land in *Asia*) to *Jerusalem* again, about seven Hours.

And so from *Jerusalem*, as the Sun goeth round the Earth to *Jerusalem* again, are 24 Hours, that is, from the Sun-setting at *Jerusalem* the 11th of *March*, 169¾. to the Sun-setting at *Jerusalem* the 12th of *March*, 169¾. are 17 Hours from *Jerusalem* to *Japan*, and 7 Hours from *Japan* to *Jerusalem*, and 17 and 7 are 24 Hours, the Evening and the Morning which make up the Day.

Which Scheme does, as I weakly can, travel round the World, and if it be right in the main, may answer some Doubts about the Days in this case. And if I mistake, I think I do not wilfully mistake, in which account I had no help from Globes, and so I have no great assurance, but that there may be mistakes, and I am content to be corrected by the Learned Doctor, who excels in Astronomy, in Geography, and I think in most other Learning. Or any other Ingenious, Unprejudiced and Skilful, who may find mistakes in the Degrees of Longitude, and in the Hours or Minutes, which however I think may not hurt the Opinion built upon it, that the difference in the time of the Sun setting in any of, and all those places, and so of all other places in the Earth, the 11 of *March*, 169¾. makes no alteration in the beginning or ending of the Sabbath day, supposing as before, that day (with the rest of the Days of the Week) did begin at the Creation, and does still begin and end about the time of the Sun setting, and suppose also that beginning and ending never altered since the Creation to this day.

And if this be so, it seems demonstrable, that every Day of the Week began every where in the Evening, and so the Seventh day also round the World as the Sun did set.

L The

The Doctor's other expedient, *he would have me begin my Week on Monday, and then Sunday will be the Seventh day,* I suppose he means if I can tell seven. But if the Doctor please to begin the Week as God begins it, *Gen.* 1. 5. and if he reckon on *v.* 8. 13, 19, 23, 31. as God does, he will find *Gen.* 2. 2, 3. the Seventh day to be the Sabbath, and as it seems to me, to begin in the Evening.

And in lieu of his two Expedients, I will with his Favour, advise him and others two things,

1st. Upon the Fourth Command, *Exod.* 20. 8, 9. *To take heed how they assume a liberty to alter any Command of God, or any jot or tittle thereof,* because of *Mat.* 5. 18, 19. & *Rev.* 22. 18, 19, &c.

2dly. Upon the Second Command; *Whatever be the manner of Worship in the place where he or they live, unless they be sure that for Matter and Manner it be according to Christs Institutions: That they beware how they take it as they there find it, which though it may be a probable means of worldly Advantages, yet* I have some doubt, it is no sound Rule to Worship by, because *the Lord thy God is a jealous God, visiting iniquity,* &c. *and shewing mercy to those who love him, and keep his commandments,* Exod. 20. 4, 5, 6. & Deut. 5. 8, 9, 10, &c.

And upon the whole, I think not A, but the Seventh-day-Sabbath was observed by the Lord, *Gen.* 2. 2, 3. and afterward by the Patriarchs, by *Moses*, and by the *Israelites* in *Ægypt*, and in the Wilderness of *Sin*, where they had *Mannah*, and at *Mount Synai*, and at *Mount Zion* in *Jerusalem*, and to the end of the Old Testament, *to whom the Lord made known his sabbath,* Neh. 9. 13, 14. his Sabbaths as before, *and to whom he gave them as a sign, and as an everlasting covenant, and that not A, but,* The Sabbath *was observed perfectly and constantly by* Christ *during his life,* which I think proves it not forgotten, nor altered to his time, and that not A, but The Sabbath was observed by his Disciples, inspired by the Holy Spirit after his Resurrection, and Ascension, which also proves it not forgotten, nor altered then.

And as their losing the Knowledge, which was the Seventh day, is not in the Word that I know, so the certain Seventh day, was preserved by all Nations, Worshipping the Sun on Sunday, Mr. *Chafie,* p. 20, &c. *and all the* Israelites *before Christ, and all the* Jews *since* (that we can read or hear of) *and some Christians still keep not* A, *but* The Seventh day, *and many Christians keep the first day, other Christians keep both Seventh and First day,* as in the *Enquiry*; and the early and long Controversies about what Days to keep the Passover on, and the Histories, Counsels, Centuries, and our own Records, Ancient and

Modern,

Modern, as in the *Enquiry*, seem plainly to prove, that the Seventh day was never altered, from Chrifts time to this day, nor from the Creation to Chrifts time, and that the Seventh day in *England* is the fame Seventh day varying the Hours and Minutes as before, which was obferved by Chrift, which was made perpetual by Chrift, which was obferved at *Mount Zion*, which was given at *Synai*, and *which was bleft and made holy at the Creation*, Gen. 2.

And here I might alfo obferve, that the Doctor neither denys nor anfwers the Authorities in the *Enquiry*, for obferving the Sabbath, 400 and 700 years, &c. after Chrift, and for the changing the Seventh day to the Firft day by *Rome*, &c. nor the clear Evidence for the firft bringing in the Firft day into *Scotland*, by a Counfel there above 1200 years after Chrift, nor that of the King and Nobles of *England* here to like purpofe, *Enquiry* p. 106. to 114, &c.

Nor that how all our Antient and Modern Records in *England* to this day, call the Seventh day of the Week the Sabbath day, *Enquiry*, p. 117. to which the Doctor fays nothing, nor to that of the many Provinces and one Empire ftill obferving the Seventh day, *Enq.* p. 119, 120. And all put together, I think may fufficiently difprove the uncertainty which is the Seventh day, which the Doctor fo often would leave doubtful againft himfelf, and may prove that our Seventh day of the Week is the true Seventh day, *bleffed and made holy at the creation*.

And I infift, that Chrifts Command to keep Holy the Seventh day, not being altered, nor repealed, but with all the reft confirmed, and made perpetual by him, ftill binds, as all the reft of the Commands do.

I have paffed by divers Expreffions in the Doctor's Book, but have not that I know declined any thing that required, as I think, further Reply, and what he objects again, and again I often think it enough to anfwer to but once. And if I do not fully repeat his Objections or Words at large, it is to make this Reply as fhort as I can, and the Reader may refort to the Book.

And to conclude: Inftead of further fumming up what I have weakly written here in Reply to the Learned Doctor and others, as I could, I commend to the Reader a few Scriptures.

Gen. 2. 2, 3, 4. *On the seventh day God ended his work which he had made, and he rested the seventh day from all his work which he had made, and God blessed the seventh day, and made it holy, because that in it he had rested from all his work which he had created and made;*

and so the Sabbath is the day upon which God rested after his Work, and which he Blessed and made Holy, who is, *v.* 4. *Jehovah Ælohim*, the Lord God, so the Seventh day is the Lords day.

Exod. 16. 29. *The seventh-day-sabbath is said to be as it is, a gift, The Lord hath given you the sabbath*, and so we should take it as a Gift from him, as his Gift, and as the Lords day.

Exod. 20. 8, 9, 10, 11. *Remember the sabbath day to keep it holy*, &c. *The seventh day is the sabbath of the Lord thy God*, and so the Seventh day is the Lords day.

Exod. 31. 13. The Lord calls them *my sabbaths, verily, my sabbaths ye shall keep*, so the Sabbath is the Lords day, *it is a sign between me and you*, &c. *that ye may know that I am the Lord that doth sanctifie you*, v. 14. *and ye shall keep the sabbath because it is holiness to you*, v. 15. *Six days work shall be done, but the seventh is the sabbath of rest, holiness to the Lord*, v. 16. *the sabbath, a perpetual covenant, tis holiness to you*, v. 14. *and holy to the Lord*, v. 15. & v. 16. *the sabbath, a perpetual covenant*, and v. 17. *a sign for ever. For in six days the Lord made heaven and earth, and on the seventh day he rested, and was refreshed*, so the Seventh day is the Lords day. And v. 18. *The Lord gave to Moses two tables of testimony, written with the finger of God.* And Exod. 32. 15, 16. *the tables were the work of God, and the writing the writing of God*, upon which tables of testimony or witness the fourth command was one.

Exod. 35. 2. *Six days shall work be done, and on the seventh day it shall be to you holiness.*

Lev. 23. 3. *Six days shall work be done, but the seventh day is the sabbath of rest, an holy convocation, ye shall do no work therein, it is the sabbath of the Lord*, &c. so the Seventh day is the Lords day.

Lev. 23. 32. *from even unto even shall ye celebrate your sabbath*, which I think is directing in an Humiliation day, which is there to begin in the Evening when they were to afflict themselves.

And I think states this part of the Question, when the Days began, that is, in the Evening, and when they ended, that is, at the next Evening, which the Dr. p. 27. thinks, began and ended at mid-night.

In *Numb.* 15. 32. we have the case of the Man who gathered sticks not A, but The Sabbath day, which is a great, certain, undeniable example against the least prophaning of the Sabbath day.

Deut. 5. 12. *Keep the sabbath day to sanctifie it, as the Lord thy God hath commanded thee,* 13. *Six days labour*, &c. v. 14. *But the seventh day is the sabbath of the Lord thy God*, &c. so the Seventh day

day is the Lords day of Rest (*i.e.*) *the seventh day is the Lords day*, Psal. 119. 1, 6. *blessed are those who walk in his law, and in keeping of his commandments there is great reward*, Psal. 19. 11.

Esai. 56. 2. *Blessed is the man who keepeth the sabbath from polluting it*, v. 4. 6. *from polluting it*, Ezek. 20. 13, 16, 24. *my sabbath they greatly polluted*, if we would be Blessed, keep his Sabbaths, and dont pollute them, which it seems was *Israels* Sin, of old.

Esai. 58. 13. *If thou turn away thy foot from the sabbath, from doing thy pleasure on my holy day, and call the sabbath a delight, or delights, the holy of the Lord* (so the Sabbath day is the Lords day) *honourable, and shalt honour him, not doing thine own ways, nor finding thine own pleasure, nor speaking thine own words*, v. 14. *then shalt thou delight thy self in the Lord*, &c. and is not that a desirable frame?

Ezek. 22. 1, 2. *The word of the Lord, thou hast prophaned my sabbath*, v. 26. *her Priests have violated my law, &c. and have hid their eyes from my sabbaths*. So the Sabbath day is the Lords day.

Ezek. 44. 4, 5, 15, 24. *in the prophesie of the new temple there is a promise, that the Priests who shall come near unto the Lord to minister unto him, they shall hallow my sabbaths*. So the Sabbath day is the Lords day.

Matth. 5. 17. *Think not that I am come to destroy the law*, v. 18. *For verily I say unto you, till heaven and earth pass, one jot, or one tittle shall in no wise pass from the law, till all be fulfilled*, dont think that Christ altered one tittle of the Law, and so not one jot or tittle is yet passed from the Law.

Matth. 18. 8. Christ is said to be Lord of the Sabbath day, and if Christ be Lord of the Sabbath day, then the Sabbath day is the Lords day.

Mat. 24. 20. *Pray that your flight be not on the sabbath day*, which flight was about 38 years after Christs Death, which I think shews it was to continue after his Death, that is, as I think, as long as the World lasts.

Matth. 28. 18, 19, 20. Christ to his Disciples, *go teach all nations, teaching them to observe all things, whatsoever I have commanded you*, and Christ with the Father and holy Spirit, one *Jehovah*, gave the commands as before.

Mark 1. 21. after Christs Baptism by *John*, v. 9. *Jesus came into Galilee, preaching the Gospel of the Kingdom of God*, v. 14. *repent ye, and believe the Gospel*, v. 15. then he calls Simon, and Andrew,
James

James and John, and they followed him, v. 16 to 20. and they went into Capernaum, and straitway, on the sabbath day, he entered into the Synagogue, and taught, and Mark 2. 27. the sabbath was made for man, for his good, for his spiritual good.

Mark 16. 1, 2. *Jesus came into his own country and his disciples followed him, and when the sabbath day was come, he began to preach in the synagogue*, which also proves the Sab. made for the spiritual use of man.

Luke 4. 16, to 27. in *v.* 14. (after his being tempted, *v.* 13.) *Jesus returned in the power of the spirit, into Galilee,* and *v.* 15. *taught in their Synagogues,* and *v.* 16. *he came to* Nazareth, *where he had been brought up, and as his custom was, he went into the Synagogue on the sabbath day, and stood up for to read,* and preached the Gospel, v. 17, to 29. *and then he came down to* Capernaum, *and taught them on the sabbath day,* besides divers other places in the Evangelists, which do all prove the Sabbath made for the spiritual good of Man. And so I think we have enough to prove that our Lord Jesus Christ kept the Sabbath during his life, and that perfectly; *for he was a lamb without spot or blemish,* 1 Pet. 1. 19, &c. and that the Seventh day Sabbath was made holy for the spiritual Good of Man.

Luke 16. 17. it is easier for Heaven and Earth to pass, then one tittle of the Law to fail, which one would think are strong words, and of Authority in this case. And Heaven and Earth are not yet passed, and so not one tittle of the Law does yet fail; and if this Scripture be true, as it surely is, it mightily proves the Seventh day to be the Sabbath, *Exod.* 20. 10. which Seventh day in the Fourth Command is more then a tittle.

Luke 23. 54, 55, 56. And when he was Crucified, Dead and Buried, and the Sabbath drew on, the Women followed after, and beheld the Sepulchre, and how his Body was laid, and they returned and prepared Spices and Ointments, and rested, not A, but The Sabbath day, according to the Commandment, that is, according to the Fourth Commandment, and so the Seventh day was not altered then, and so kept not A, but the Sabbath day, after Christs Death and Burial, as in probability all other Believers then did, for I do not remember to have read of any that deny it.

John 14. 15. *If ye love me keep my commandments,* Exod. 20. 6. Deut. 7. 9 John 14. 21. *he that hath my commandments and keepeth them, he it is that loveth me,* 23. *If a man love me he will keep my words.*

John 15. 10. *If ye keep my commandments ye shall abide in my love,* 14. *ye are my friends, if ye do whatsoever I command you.* Are we Friends of Christ, and would we abide in his Love, then keep his Commands.

Acts

Acts 13. 13, 14. *Paul* and his Company went into the Synagogue at *Antioch* on the Sabbath day, and *v.* 15. *After the reading of the law and the prophets*, v. 16. Paul *stood up and preached Christ* to them, from v. 16. to 41. and, v. 42. the Gentiles besought that these words might be preached to them the next Sabbath, not the next Morning upon the First day of the Week, but the next Sabbath, and so after the Resurrection and Ascension of Christ, and after the Disciples were all filled with the Holy Spirit, *Acts* 2. 1, 4. Tis certain *Paul* kept the Sabbath, and Preached to Jews and Gentiles, not upon the First day of the Week, but upon the Sabbath day.

And we have the like. *Acts* 13. 44. the next Sabbath day (not the next Morning) almost the whole City came together to hear the Word of God, and v. 47, 48. *as many of the gentiles as were ordained to eternal life believed*: so divers Gentiles were here converted unto Christ on the Sabbath day, v. 49. *the word of the Lord was published throughout all the region*, and v. 52. *the disciples were filled with joy, and with the holy spirit*, and is not this a desirable frame? and doe not all these prove that the Sabbath was made for the spiritual good of Man?

And *Acts* 14, 1. In *Iconium*, *Paul* and *Barnabas* went both together into the Synagogue of the Jews, and so spake, that a great multitude both of the *Jews*, and also of the *Greeks* believed, a great multitude, and v. 3. *The Lord gave testimony to the world of his grace, by signs and wonders done by them*. *Acts* 16. 1, 3, 12, 13, 14, 15. at *Philippi*, *Paul* and *Timothy*, on the Sabbath day went out of the City by a Rivers side, where Prayer was wont to be made, and spake to the women which resorted thither, where *Lydia* was converted, whose heart the Lord opened, that she attended unto the things which were spoken of *Paul*, and was baptized, and her Houshold; which Scriptures with many others, do shew, and I think prove that the Sabbath was not altered, but did continue after Christs Ascension, and was observed.

Acts 17. 1. to 4. at *Thessalonica*, where was a Synagogue of the Jews, Paul, as his manner was (as Christs manner was *Luke* 4. 16.) went in unto them, and three *sabbath days reasoned with them out of the scriptures*, alledging, that Christ must needs have suffered, and risen again from the Dead, and that this Jesus whom he preach'd unto them is Christ, and some of them believed, and consorted with *Paul* and *Silas*, and of the devout Greeks, that is of the Gentiles, a great multitude, and of the the chief Women, not a few

were

were converted to Christ upon the Sabbath day, so the Law for keeping Holy the Sabbath, was not then passed away.

And *Acts* 18. 1, 2, 4, 5, 19. at *Corinth Paul* Reasoned, that is (*Greek*) Preached in the Synagogue every Sabbath, and perswaded the Jews and the Greeks, that is, the Jews and Gentiles. And what greater, and stronger, and clearer Evidence and Proof for the Seventh-day-Sabbath can Man desire, then these plain Scriptures are? and that it was at first Instituted, Blessed, and made Holy, and throughout the Scriptures of Old and New Testament, used for the conversion and eternal good of Man.

Rom. 3. 31. *Do we then make void the law through Faith, be it not, yea, we establish the law.* Rom. 7. 12. *The law is holy, and just, and good.* Rom. 7. 14. *we know that the Law is Spiritual.* Rom. 10. 4. *Christ is the end of the Law for righteousness, to every one that believeth.* And 1 Cor. 9. 21. Paul *was under the law to Christ,* and 1 Cor. 11. 1. he saith, *be ye followers of me, even as I also am of Christ,* who 1 Cor. 15. 3. *dyed for our sins,* and 1 John 3. 4. *sin is the transgression of the law,* but Gal. 3. 11. *no man is justified by the law,* v. 13. *Christ hath redeemed us from the curse of the Law,* v. 21. *Is the law against the promises of God, God forbid,* or be it not, v. 24. but *our schoolmaster unto Christ, that we might be justified by faith;* who Tit. 2. 14. *gave himself for us, that he might redeem us from all anomy, or contrariety* (in Opinion or Conversation) *to the law of God,* and Heb. 8. 10. the Lord saith, *I will put my laws into their minds, and write them in or upon their hearts,* which surely is greatly desirable, that his Law be written on our Hearts. And we have the like promise, Heb. 10. 15, 16, 17. saith the Lord, *I will put my laws into their hearts, and in their minds will I write them,* which Law in *Jam.* 20. 8. is called a Royal Law, that is, the Kingly, Chief, and universal Law, under which all other Laws of God are comprehended, which Christ, the Lord and King over all, hath prescribed and commanded, 1 *John* 1. 10. *If we say that we have not sinned, we make him a liar,* 1 John 2. 3. *and hereby we know that we know him, if we keep his commandments,* v. 4. *he that saith I know him, and keepeth not his commandments* (is mistaken) v. 6. *he that saith he abideth in him, ought himself so to walk, even as he walked,* and Christ kept the Sabbath, and 1 John 3. 22. *whatsoever we ask, we receive of him, because we keep his commandments,* and 1 John 5. 3. *for this is the love of God, that we keep his commandments,* 2 Ep. of Joh 6. *this is love, that we walk after his commandments,* Rev. 12. 17. *The Dragon was wroth, and went to make War with those who kept the Commandments of God, and have the Testimony of Jesus Christ,* and *Rev.* 14. 12. *Here are those who keep the commandments of God, and the faith of Jesus,* and Rev. 22. 14. *Blessed are they that do his commandments, that they may have right to the tree of life, and may enter through the gates into the city.*

FINIS.

ERRATA.

PAge 3. line 28. *for Cronologies*, read *Cronologers*, p. 4. l. 5. r. *one*, p. 5. l. 15. for *v.* 19. r. *v.* 16. p. 5. l. 39. r. *but*, p. 9. l 27. *dele and*, p. 10. l. 15. *for Jashebeth*, r. *Lashebeth*, p. 12. l. 15. *for Morah*, r. *Marah*, p. 13. l. 14. *dele* 22. l. 15. *for* Exod. 12. 12, 13. r. Exod. 12. 32. p. 15. l. 4. *for* 23. r. 2, 3. p. 16. l. 28. *for* 15. r. 14. p. 18. l. 37. *dele* 14. p. 19. l. 26. *for v.* 5. r. *v.* 6. p. 21. l. 1. *dele* & 42. p. 23. l. 18. *for* 6. r. 16. l. 21. *dele* & 21. 46. p. 24. l. 23. *for one*, r. *One*, p. 29. l. 40. *for* Num. 6. r. Num. 9. p. 33. l. 5. *for* 30. r. 13. l. 35. *for* 30. r. 13. p. 34. l. 18. *dele it*, p. 41. l. 23. *for sacrificis*, r. *and sacrifices*, p. 46. l. 6. *for* σαββάτου, r. σαββάτων, l. 7. *for* σαββάτων, r. σαββάτων, p. 47. l. 6. *for* 15. r. 5. *and for* σαββάσι, σαββάσι, l. 8. *for* σαββάτων, r. σαββάτων, l. 9. *for* σαββάτων, r. σαββάτων, l. 17. *for must be, one*, r. *must be, are*, p. 49. l. 32. *dele and*, p. 50. l. 6. *for Apostles*, r. *Apostle*, l. 9. *for day*, r. *days*, l. 14. *for other*, r. *others*, p. 53. l. 11. *for was*, r. *is*, p. 54. l. 34. *for ?* put , p. 58. l. 21. *for Anp*, r. *And*, l. 26. *dele as*, p. 63. l. 31. *for His* r. *Tis*, p. 64. l. 17. *for or*, r. *of*. l. 23. *for bis*, r. *'tis*, p. 65. l. 20. r. *as before and hereafter*, p. 72. l. 30. r. *degrees*.

CPSIA information can be obtained at www.ICGtesting.com
Printed in the USA
BVOW06s0303250314

348598BV00009BB/497/P

9 781171 258254